JOHN PAUL II, WE LOVE YOU!

September 2009

Dear Sally,

We love you deeply!
The little book is a blessing!
So are you. Love, Sean & ???

John Paul II, We Love You!
Young People Encounter the Pope

Peter Mitchell

SERVANT
BOOKS

PUBLISHED BY ST. ANTHONY MESSENGER PRESS
CINCINNATI, OHIO

Cover design by Candle Light Studios
Cover photo of John Paul II by Getty Images/Francois Lochon
Book design by Phillips Robinette, O.F.M.

LIBRARY OF CONGRESS CATALOGING-IN-PUBLICATION DATA

Mitchell, Peter, 1974-
  John Paul II, we love you : young people encounter the Pope / Peter
Mitchell.
      p. cm.
  Includes bibliographical references.
  ISBN 978-0-86716-806-8 (pbk. : alk. paper) 1. John Paul II, Pope,
1920-2005—Death and burial. I. Title.

BX1378.5.M575 2007
282.092—dc22
[B]

                        2007020068

ISBN 0-978-0-86716-806-8

Published by Servant Books, an imprint of St. Anthony Messenger Press
28 W. Liberty St.
Cincinnati, OH 45202
www.ServantBooks.org

Printed in the United States of America
Printed on acid-free paper

07 08 09 10 11 6 5 4 3 2 1

To my grandmother, Pauline Mitchell (1914–2005), and to all the young people whom I have ever known as a seminarian and priest, and especially the young people of Dwight and Bee, Nebraska

Dearest little sister, Saint Thérèse, I entrust to you each one of the young people whom God has willed that my life touch. Give to each one of them, dearest Little Flower of Carmel, a deep knowledge of God's will for them, and the courage and strength to carry it out. In particular I recommend to you those for whom I now pray…

Saint Thérèse, my Carmelite Sister, I promise to make known your Little Way by word and action. Grant that I may serve God faithfully as a holy priest, and so come one day with you, our Mother Mary, and all the saints, to the joy of the heavenly wedding banquet.

Saint Thérèse, my Carmelite Sister, intercede for me.

—*Prayer written and prayed daily by the author*

Contents

Preface

"The Church is young!" These were the words of Pope Benedict XVI at his solemn Mass of installation. This truth was made unmistakably clear to the Church and to the whole world through the events of the momentous days in Rome in April 2005, when Pope John Paul the Great passed from this life to the next. As Pope Benedict described them, "During those sad days of the pope's illness and death, it became wonderfully evident to us that the Church is alive. And the Church is young."[1]

This book is about the joy and sadness of those days, as witnessed personally by a young American priest whom God's Providence happened to favor with the grace of being "in the right place at the right time." I am a priest of the "JPII generation," one of a countless number of young American priests today who trace their vocations to hearing the call of Christ at Mile High Stadium in Denver through the words and presence of John Paul II at World Youth Day 1993.

I was ordained in 1999 by Bishop Fabian W. Bruskewitz of the diocese of Lincoln, and for three years worked in parish ministry, taught high school religion and served as chaplain at the Newman Center at the

University of Nebraska. I attended the World Youth Days in Paris 1997, Rome 2000 and Toronto 2002, helping as a chaperone and spiritual guide to the youth on our diocesan pilgrimages. Throughout these years youth ministry took up the majority of my waking hours in some way, shape or form.

Then in 2002 I was sent to Rome by my bishop to pursue a doctorate in Church History at the Pontifical Gregorian University. For three years I was privileged to attend Mass with the Holy Father frequently, to assist in distributing Holy Communion at his Masses in St. Peter's Basilica and to be a firsthand witness of the suffering pontiff's final years in the Chair of Peter. There was *never* a moment when being in his presence became routine or normal. I knew that John Paul II was marking my priesthood in a way that would shape and form it forever.

In the spring of 2003, ten years after Denver, my family and I had the privilege of being introduced to Pope John Paul in his private library in the Vatican. That morning, knowing I would have just a few seconds to speak to the man who was and is my hero, I prayed intensely about what I should say to him. So many thoughts rolled through my head—but in the end I knew that I had to tell him just one thing and one thing only. As my parents, sisters and I were introduced to him, I knelt in front of him and told him, "Holy Father, I was in *Denver* at World Youth Day." "Denver…" he said back, "…I remember!" And then with tears in my eyes and the biggest, proudest smile I ever smiled, I said, "And I listened to you, and I became a priest!" "*Ve…ry…gooood*," the pope replied, and he blessed me on my forehead and gave me one of his rosaries.

I have told this story of a proud and grateful son encountering his spiritual father more times than I can possibly remember, and a photo of this moment is prominently displayed in my rectory. I so wanted him to know that after all that time I was still listening and praying and struggling to follow Christ the way he had asked me to. *He* is the reason I left everything and became a priest. Period.

Fast-forward to April 2005. I had been scheduled to leave Rome for the United States during the first week of April to begin a pastoral assignment in my diocese. When the pope died on April 2, my bishop gave me permission to stay for the funeral and conclave. God's providence had brought me face-to-face with history. Had the pope died even a week later, I would already have departed Rome and this book would never have been written.

This book exists because of a call I felt from God during those unprecedented days to share with as many people as possible the incredible things I was seeing and experiencing. I felt that the best way I could express my gratitude to God for allowing me to be there in person was to use the gift of writing to help others experience through my eyes what they could not see for themselves.

These journal entries were not written without sacrifice. Almost every one of my accounts was written in the wee hours of the morning just after the events had actually happened. I didn't want to postpone the writing, because if I did I knew that not only would my account lose its fresh vividness but also there was a good chance I would never find the time. So for the duration of those days I became one incredibly sleep-deprived, emotionally drained and physically exhausted scoop reporter.

I never sent them to anyone besides the people in my personal e-mail address book, about one hundred people. But because the events described were so dramatic, they were rapidly passed around the world via e-mail forwarding again and again and again. Somehow they took on a life of their own, and soon I began receiving them back from people I had never even heard of!

The idea for incorporating personal testimonies from young people into my journal came from Cindy Cavnar at Servant Books. I credit her with the idea and initiative for making this book happen. Writing a book is a daunting task for anyone, let alone a pastor of two parishes. But by the grace of God and the help and support of my parents, family and many, many friends, it gradually took shape. I wish also to thank Aine Gianoli for her amazing dedication in compiling and editing the final manuscript.

God's Providence was again at work in making the deadline for this book fall on All Saints' Day. As I sit here in my country rectory looking out at the November sky, the grain trucks are rolling by carrying this year's corn harvest from the Nebraska farmland. The Lord Jesus himself tells us in the Gospels that the harvest is ready, a harvest of saints for his kingdom. John Paul II was one of the greatest laborers that Christ ever called into his service, and by his life and witness he has raised up a harvest of saints for the kingdom of heaven, a harvest whose magnitude is only just beginning to be seen. This book is a testimony to a few of the first fruits of that harvest. I know that I am one of them. And if this little book brings an increase to the harvest, then may Jesus Christ be praised!

> Father Peter Mitchell
> Assumption Parish
> Dwight, Nebraska
> All Saints' Day 2006

CHAPTER ONE

The Vigil

I have looked for you; you have come to me, and I thank you.

—John Paul II[1]

Friday, April 1, 2005—ROME

I have just returned from St. Peter's Square. To my knowledge the pope has not died. The piazza was packed with people praying, many holding candles, praying the rosary, or singing softly. I was especially touched by the quiet and peace in the square. There was a real sense among all those present that we are witnessing history, and there is also a sense of solidarity with Pope John Paul II as our spiritual father.

The crowd was mainly young people. I sat with a group of high school students from Wisconsin who were here on pilgrimage for Easter Week, all of them kneeling and praying the rosary. There was also a group of Italian students nearby sitting in a circle and singing softly. A few young women from France joined us for part of the rosary. It was so moving to see these young people and their love for the pope. One young girl, perhaps fifteen years old, began sobbing uncontrollably, and many other people were moved to tears as she cried.

At 9:00 PM several bishops led the rosary in Italian. It was interesting that the mysteries we prayed together were the new Luminous Mysteries which Pope John Paul himself created in 2002 and gave to the Church. Passages of Scripture were read, as well as quotations from the Holy Father's addresses to young people. One of the reflections quoted the Holy Father reminding young people that the path to the glory of heaven always goes along the Way of the Cross, through Calvary. The pope in these difficult hours is living the mystery of Christ's death and resurrection, which he has proclaimed so constantly and faithfully during his twenty-six years as pope.

When he appeared at his window on Easter Sunday, I was also in St. Peter's Square, and there was again a real sense that it was a powerful and historic moment. Although he did not speak, the fact that he was determined to greet and give his Easter blessing to all the pilgrims was a sign to us of his love and unwavering dedication to his mission as head of the Church. As he silently blessed the crowd, repeatedly making the Sign of the Cross, many of us had the sense we would not see him again. It was his farewell to his beloved children.

We will continue to pray through the night here as we wait for further news. Here in our house, the Casa Santa Maria (home to seventy American priests studying in Rome), there is a spirit of prayer and keeping vigil.

The Vigil

Outside our chapel there is a statue of the pope, and this evening a small candle was lit next to it, which will burn throughout the night, a symbol of our prayers, which are accompanying the Holy Father in this hour of his agony.

There is an ancient custom in the Church to pray to Saint Joseph, the foster father of Jesus, for the grace of a happy death. We believe by tradition that Saint Joseph died in Nazareth in the arms of Jesus and Mary. We are praying that the Holy Father will be given the grace of a happy and peaceful death.

It is hard to believe this is all actually happening. I have wondered what this moment would be like. I am only thirty-one—I do not remember any other pope. I entered the seminary in 1993, when I was nineteen, after attending World Youth Day in Denver. He is truly my spiritual father, as he is to so many of my generation.

Tomorrow will be an interesting day. I will write more as soon as I can.

The gathering of young people in St. Peter's Square that night outside the Holy Father's window was only a tiny fraction of the young people all over the world who were spiritually united to him during the hours of his suffering and death. Countless youth had seen him during his travels on every continent; countless youth had their hearts and souls forever marked by their encounter with him. In their own words they will now recount to us the story of their personal encounters with Pope John Paul the Great.

The Eyes of a Sniper

John Paul Mitchell, New York

Whenever I encountered our late Holy Father Pope John Paul the Great, my firmest memories are of his eyes. No matter what the venue or what his physical state, his eyes remained always constant, always loving, always piercing.

My first personal encounter with him was in the spring of 1999. It was your typical popemobile encounter. I was in Rome for spring break and got tickets to one of his Wednesday audiences. He passed by amidst a flurry of flags and banners, hands and heads. But in the chaos, I distinctly remember his eyes—picking people off as he blessed them. Like a sniper coolly connecting with a series of targets, John Paul connected with one person after another, blessing them along the way. Whether each person noticed the connection, I don't know, but the pope knew, and that was all that was necessary for grace to flow through him.

Flip forward three years to the summer of 2002 at World Youth Day in Toronto. Here I did not get so close, but again it was his eyes that I remember. He was on the JumboTron, and the crowd was chanting to him. The pope was visibly weak and was seated for his speech. In years past he might have gone up to the microphone and responded to the crowd, as he was famous for saying in Denver, "John Paul II, he loves you!" This time, he simply banged on the bookstand in front of him, in sync with the cheers. The crowd erupted, and I remember seeing the pope's eyes light up. This time, *we* had been a grace to *him*.

On a third encounter with him, I finally got an intimate look at those eyes that had so intrigued me. After a general audience in the Paul VI Audience Hall in 2002, my family and a group of students we were leading were invited up to greet the pope and receive his blessing. By this time his Parkinson's disease had taken a strong hold on his speech and physical appearance. He was hunched over in his chair and seemed rigid and slow-moving. I will never forget the string of drool he slowly wiped from his mouth as we approached. Despite all of this, his eyes were *alive*. He was deeply focused on what we were saying, and you could tell his mind was moving ten times faster than his body. There was also a twinkle in them—an unforgettable hint of mischief and of humor.

G.K. Chesterton once said, "There is a road from the eye to the heart that does not go through the intellect.

Men do not quarrel about the meaning of sunsets; they never dispute that the hawthorn says the best and wittiest thing about the spring."[2] I think Pope John Paul's eyes revealed just such an indisputable message. They led you past what your intellect was telling you about this man—that he was old and debilitated and out of it. Inside, his heart was roiling with a magma flow of love that overflowed from his eyes. There was a hidden vigor there, an internal turbine that no Parkinson's disease could impede. That turbine was Christ. And in Pope John Paul's eyes I was given the grace to encounter Christ living and breathing in the twenty-first century.

My final encounter with John Paul was shared with the world. I was sitting alone in a student lounge, watching his televised funeral. As his coffin was lifted up before St. Peter's Square for that final farewell, we could not see his eyes, but we all felt him looking out at us one last time. He looked not only out, but down from above as well—down on his children who, through his sparkling eyes, had come to know him as a father.

John Paul's gaze did not end in death, for the gaze of Christ is everlasting. Indeed, as then-Cardinal Ratzinger so wisely reassured us, "We can be sure that our beloved pope is standing today at the window of the Father's house, that he sees us and blesses us."[3]

The Pope Who Made It Real

Lori Lieb, Nebraska

It was a privilege to walk this earth during the same time as John Paul II. Gentle shepherd. Humble servant. Affectionate father. Challenging confronter. Unstoppable pilgrim. Undaunted leader. Genuine friend. This is who John Paul II was to me and to the world. Although I never met him, his very presence at the times I saw him and the multitude of photos of him made him a very real and important person in my life. As more time passes since his death, I find myself wanting to cling to my memories of him so as not to forget his powerful, beautiful, sometimes almost surreal presence.

He became pope one year and two days after I was born. I saw him for the first time fifteen years later in Denver, Colorado, the summer between my freshman and sophomore years of high school. Our group had tickets to the papal welcome at Mile High Stadium. I remember him landing in a helicopter and ascending the stage. I also remember that he talked about how Jesus needs the youth of the world—now—to make his presence known. How we shouldn't be afraid to commit our lives to Christ. "Be not afraid!"

It was an impressionable time in my own life. I was trying to make good decisions, but like most high school kids, I was nervous about living my life against the grain. I *was* afraid. Even though he was talking to thousands, his words really penetrated my heart and made me want to commit. I wanted to tell him he could count me in; I wanted to tell him I wouldn't let my fears conquer me! During Mass I remember seeing the mobs of people from all over the world joining hands to pray the Our Father. That was when I knew I wouldn't be alone in my commitment. I knew I was a part of something larger, the Catholic Church, the body of Christ.

His larger-than-life presence almost seemed too good to be true. But I watched him carefully after World Youth Day. I loved his voice. I loved the way his face wrinkled when he smiled. I was fascinated by pictures of him, stunned by his incredible acts of love and moved by his willingness to apologize on behalf of the Church. I thought, "Who is this guy? He knows how to ski. He can kayak. He embraces people from every culture. He *really* values multiculturalism—he wears traditional dress from various cultures, he accepts gifts from other nations, and he visits sites treasured by other religions."

John Paul II really loved people. He said it and he lived it. He wasn't afraid to be close to them—he kissed children with AIDS, he visited the poor and invited them to be with him, he pleaded for death row inmates, he traveled the planet making sure no one thought he or she was too small or too unimportant to be visited by the pope. He showed me that it was okay to meet people on their turf. Yet he always tried to spread the Truth also. He never compromised the teachings for which he stood.

It would be nine years before I would see him again, this time in Rome with a small group of friends. We went to his weekly audience, and again I distinctly remember his coming out onto the stage, this time on a mobilized throne of sorts. I was shocked to see him so weakened, and it made me cry to see his deteriorated body, his bloated and distorted face, his shaking hand, his frail voice. This was not the passionate leader I remembered as a teen in Denver. He was a feeble and weary old man. I felt so sad for him, that God would allow disease and old age to attack his body so fiercely, that he could no longer enjoy his days with such vigor, joy and zeal, that each day and each breath were now a struggle for him. Even though I had heard in the news that these things were happening, it was quite a shock to see them up close.

He delivered his address in various languages, and I was so disheartened because I couldn't understand more than a few words of the English he spoke. I wanted him to reenergize my faith, to challenge me again, to inspire me to change. But all I could do was watch in disbelief as our tired shepherd gave as much of his life as he had left to his precious flock.

Just two months later I would see John Paul again for the last time, this time at World Youth Day in Toronto. What a privilege to be able to help give to teens the same life-changing experience I myself had had as a teen. Based on what I had just seen in Rome, I did not have high hopes for his appearance in Toronto. But miracles do occur. I couldn't believe it. Everyone always says how much the youth energize John Paul, and I got to witness it firsthand.

The first time we saw him, amidst the hundreds of thousands of youth shouting, "John Paul II! We love you!" John Paul took the stage and said, "John Paul II, he loves you too!" Of course the crowds roared their acceptance. His voice, although still slurred, was passionate and energetic once again. His humor had returned, and his intense presence was back. I could not have been more thrilled. This was the man I wanted my students to know and cherish. I wanted them to be able to believe him when he said he loved them. I wanted them to accept his challenge to be people of the Beatitudes.

Although John Paul's health continued to deteriorate, I was still not ready for him to go. I had come to love and trust this Holy Father so much that I did not want him to leave us. I never even had met him personally, but I felt as if I did know him. He had such a personal and sincere way of speaking and smiling and joking. In the days following his death, I caught as much of the news as I could and cried whenever I watched the coverage.

It's hard to believe he is gone. I feel tremendously blessed to have been so personally affected by a man as great as he. May he be eternally rewarded for being the good and faithful servant that he was. Thanks be to God for giving us such a humble, human and faithful shepherd.

Father of Love

Paul Akre, Wisconsin

My classmates and I were three rows from the front in the Paul VI Audience Hall, smashed against the aisle. People from all over the world were entering the hall like ants trying to get as close to the aisle as possible. We all knew our beloved Pope John Paul II was going to come down that aisle. Awaiting his entrance, I had feelings of excitement, fright, happiness, anticipation and anxiety.

When he entered the hall it almost seemed that the Holy Father contained the world's strongest magnet and that each individual in the crowd was attracted to that magnet. We crushed one another to make sure we were right up against the barrier, holding out our hands, taking pictures, crying out to him as he passed. I was able to touch him as he as he went by.

I can't tell you what he said during his speech because I was lost with just being in his presence. How had I— little Paul Joseph Akre from Pewaukee, Wisconsin— received this incomprehensible opportunity? I didn't know what to think, expect or feel.

Very unexpectedly my school group was among those invited to meet the Holy Father on stage. When we approached him, I was shaking nervously, in complete awe. I didn't know what to say except, "I love you, Holy Father. You are such an inspiration to me and the rest of the world. I love you!"

For the thirty seconds that we were in his immediate presence, I just looked at him, particularly at his eyes, and I felt this sensation run throughout my entire body that I cannot describe. It seemed as if I was in a movie, and this part was in super-slow motion. Just before we were asked to move offstage, I leaned over, grabbed the Holy Father's hand and kissed it. He looked at me and another unfamiliar sensation ran from the top of my head to my toes.

I cannot recall what happened after we moved off the stage to exit the room. My memory is all a blur, and all I was saying was, "Wow!" and "Oh, my goodness!" and "What just happened?" Along with my classmates, I stood outside the hall sobbing uncontrollably. Why should we be crying with such intensity? Was that not the most beautiful experience we had ever had in our lives? For twenty minutes we stood there crying, frozen in awe. We couldn't move from the spot; we were smiling, looking at one another, laughing and crying at the same time.

The only explanation is that the Holy Spirit had just touched our lives through the Holy Father in a way we'd never before experienced.

A Love That Changed My Heart

Gina Gianoli, California

For nineteen years of my life, John Paul II was the only pope I ever knew—the Polish pope, the pope who said

"Be not afraid," the skiing pope. Even while I was little, John Paul II embodied what it meant to be Catholic, an exciting Catholic. And even when he could barely walk and could speak only with great effort, he never stopped exuding that spirit of joy and vitality. While his body was old, his brave heart was young.

I was born in the midst of his papacy in 1986, and he has had and still is having a profound impact on my life. I say *is* because, although he has now passed from this life into the next, his work in the vineyard of the Lord is just as fruitful now, if not more so, than it was while he was still with us. I feel that this man, through his teachings and writings and his loving embrace for the youth, has been one of the Lord's greatest instruments. John Paul II has inspired my heart to not take the easy path, but to take the road less traveled and to step out into the deep.

Ever since I was very small, my family has had the Eternal Word Television Network in our house, so I was able to see the Holy Father often and watch him say Mass. I watched him travel around the world reaching out to all people. My sister went to World Youth Day in Denver in 1993. I was too young to go, but I watched on TV and dreamed about meeting that exciting guy who danced on the stage in his white cassock. To me, he was the epitome of cool.

I had my heart set on attending World Youth Day in Toronto, but it was so soon after the horrific events of September 11, 2001, that my parents thought it too risky, and I agreed. My family and I again watched the events on EWTN, filled with joy. In the eyes of the world it looked foolish—thousands of young people cheering, shouting and crying over an old man who by this time could barely walk. But with the gift of faith, the true beauty of what was happening could be fathomed. Beneath the white hair and wrinkles was a man who had opened his heart to God and was free. Through his openness, the Lord was able to use him to touch the hearts of so many who were seeking the truth.

After seeing World Youth Day on TV, I wanted to meet the pope more than ever. I continued to pray for him, and I trusted that the Lord's will would be done. Two years after World Youth Day in Toronto, I had the opportunity to travel in Europe with my sister and a friend. Our first stop: Rome. Our first glimpse of John Paul II was from St. Peter's Square.

The Holy Father came to the window of his residence at noon for the Sunday Angelus, and he gave us his blessing. My heart was deeply moved as I knelt with hundreds of people around me on the cobblestones in the square. I felt like the pope had spoken directly to me. I felt small and alone. I could have burst with joy, and I cannot explain why. Nothing out of the ordinary had happened, yet I knew I would not be the same again.

We saw him two more times from his window and again at a weekly audience, where we were able to sit as close as the seventh row. We could see him very clearly.

He spoke feebly, but with such love and conviction that I was moved to tears, although I cannot remember a word he said. A severe case of food poisoning made it difficult for the three of us even to sit up straight. The illness made me feel closer to John Paul, however, and I thanked God for the opportunity to offer up my small amount of suffering for the intentions of the Vicar of Christ, who was plainly in very great pain.

I prayed for the pope as we traveled throughout other European countries, and at the end of our journey we again visited Rome. It was the night before Palm Sunday Mass, which we planned to attend in St. Peter's Square, when we heard a rap on the door of our room in the convent where we were staying. One of the sisters came in and presented us with three tickets. We did not know what they were for exactly. The next day we took them to a Swiss Guard who ushered us to the bronze doors where we, with about seventy other people, were given eight-foot-long palm branches. Carrying the palms, we walked behind priests, bishops and cardinals through the crowds of people in the square to the altar where the Holy Father sat. At the top of the stairs leading to the altar, we each stopped in front of the pope, who sat about ten feet back. He raised his hand to give his blessing.

His hand shook, but I barely noticed, for his eyes were fixed upon me. His eyes were beautiful and young. In them I could see a love like no other. That love looked inside of my heart. I forgot to bow and was forced to move on, but at the same time I vowed that I would not refuse the Lord in whatever he asked me to do, because the love that flowed from John Paul was the Love that calls all people. It was the love of Christ, and it captured my heart.

When the Holy Father passed away, I got up in the middle of the night to watch the funeral Mass from my college residence, weeping from sadness, joy and thankfulness. Sadness that he is no longer here to embrace us, encourage us and love us as he did for so long. Joy that he is in heaven and can now do even more for us. And thankfulness that he was our pope and that I have been blessed to be part of the John Paul II generation. I pray to him every day, hoping that perhaps now he knows my name. When I study I ask for his prayers. When I play soccer I ask for his help. When I make mistakes I ask for his humor. His life changed my life, and his love changed my heart.

CHAPTER TWO

The Passing

In the name of Jesus Christ crucified and risen, in the spirit of His messianic mission, enduring in the history of humanity, we raise our voices and pray that the Love which is in the Father may once again be revealed at this stage of history, and that, through the work of the Son and Holy Spirit, it may be shown to be present in our modern world and to be more powerful than evil: more powerful than sin and death.

—John Paul II, *Dives in Misericordia*[1]

Saturday, April 2, 2005—ROME

After a day of quiet and prayerful waiting we have finally received word of the Holy Father's passing. John Paul II is dead. It seems impossible that I am writing these words. This whole day has seemed surreal. My glimpse of it is as follows:

After leaving St. Peter's Square at midnight last night, I was back at 6:15 this morning. I woke up and could not sleep and decided the best place to be was near the pope, both physically as well as in spirit. The square was quite empty at that early hour. A few pilgrims held a sign that said, in Polish, "We are with you." Some Italians sang quietly and prayed the rosary.

At 7:00 AM I went into St. Peter's Basilica and celebrated Mass at the altar of Saint Pius X, who was pope from 1903 to 1914. I began Mass with three people attending and ended with a group of several dozen people gathered around the altar. As it was First Saturday, I especially entrusted the pope to the care of Our Lady of Fatima, who asked that the first Saturday of the month be especially dedicated to her Immaculate Heart. It was on the anniversary of the apparition of Mary at Fatima, on May 13, 1981, that John Paul II survived the assassination attempt on his life, and the pope had attributed his survival to her.

Yesterday on my way down to St. Peter's Square, I found myself walking next to an Italian priest, and he said to me, "Today is First Friday; he will go to the Lord today." And I responded, "Perhaps," but it dawned on me at that moment how fitting it would be in God's Providence if the Lord took John Paul to himself through Mary's hands on her special day, First Saturday.

The rest of the morning and early afternoon were spent at home with the radio on. There were no announcements about the pope's condition for most of the day, and gradually we realized that this meant there would be no news until the announcement we were all waiting for would be made.

At 4:00 PM I attended a Mass celebrated by Francis Cardinal Arinze of Nigeria in the parish Church of St. Anne, which is located in Vatican City, literally in the shadow of the papal apartments. I joined the cardinal in praying for the pope and also for seven young people from Wisconsin, including my youngest sister Maria, who received the sacrament of confirmation from the cardinal. They had scheduled this Mass with him and reserved the church months ago, and in God's Providence they found themselves at the center of history in the making. In the sacristy after the Mass I helped sign and stamp the certificates of confirmation, all stamped with the Vatican seal and dated April 2, 2005. They must have been the last seven people confirmed during the pontificate of John Paul II.

By 6:00 PM we returned to the square, which by now was so jammed with people that it seemed like the crowd that had gathered for Easter last Sunday had multiplied itself ten times over. Cameras, microphones and reporters swarmed all over the square, while the crowd sang, prayed and waited.

I went out to a dinner held in honor of the young people who had been confirmed. We were on our way back toward St. Peter's when we heard the news that the pope had died at 9:37 PM Rome time. I was actually standing at a bus stop on the Appian Way, a few hundred meters from the catacombs of Saint Callistus, built in the third century AD and holding the tombs of several of the ancient popes, including Saint Fabian, Saint Sixtus and Saint Zephyrinus. I led the young students in prayer for our deceased Holy Father as we waited for the bus, thinking that John Paul II must now be in the company of those great pontiffs from the ancient Church.

Taking the bus back to the Vatican took quite a while, as we expected. We were jammed onto a bus and stuck in heavy traffic. The students, all between the ages of fourteen and seventeen, prayed the rosary aloud on the bus and sang hymns to Mary and Jesus. Their devotion was inspiring and obviously impressive to the array of Italians and tourists on the bus. Most of them were either silent or quietly joining us in prayer—not the scene one typically encounters while riding the Roman bus and subway system!

We eventually got off the bus and started walking because traffic had come to a near-standstill in central Rome. We arrived at St. Peter's Square at about 11:30 PM. The entire Via della Conciliazione, which leads into the square, was a mass of humanity. People were covering the square, some kneeling, other sitting wrapped in blankets, others walking or staring at the windows of the papal apartments, which looked the same as last night—but now the pope is no longer there, only his body.

A prayer service began shortly after midnight. The Scripture readings were taken from the Feast of Divine

Mercy, which is celebrated on the Sunday after Easter and was made a feast day by John Paul II, taking his inspiration from Saint Faustina Kowalska, a Polish nun and mystic who lived in Krakow before her death in 1937. The double coincidence that the pope has died on a First Saturday and on the vigil of the Feast of Divine Mercy, which he instituted, is truly remarkable. I take it as a sign that the Lord chose the exact moment when he wanted to take John Paul II to himself.

At one point in the prayer service, one of the bishops asked everyone to lift a round of applause up to the heavens. This is an Italian custom when expressing grief and love for someone who has departed this life. The entire piazza began clapping and sustained this applause vigorously for almost ten minutes. It was quite remarkable. Toward the end of the applause, some young people began the favorite chant, "Giovanni Paolo!" and soon the entire square was calling out the name of our beloved father. The crowd then joined together in singing the Our Father in Italian. The prayer service concluded with the singing of the "Salve Regina" in Latin, an ancient hymn to Mary asking that "after this our exile" she will "show unto us the blessed fruit of thy womb Jesus," a prayer that I know has been answered on this night for John Paul II. A light shone on the icon of Mary and the Christ child, which John Paul himself put in the square after the assassination attempt in 1981.

About a block from St. Peter's Square, all-night adoration of the Blessed Sacrament is being held at the Church of the Holy Spirit on the Borgo Santo Spirito. Exactly ten years ago, on Divine Mercy Sunday 1995, Pope John Paul dedicated this seventeenth-century church as the Sanctuary of Divine Mercy in Rome. Some time after midnight I squeezed in the back of the church—the floor was completely covered with people praying and crying—and attended part of a Mass. At the moment of the customary prayer for the pope during the eucharistic prayer of the Mass, there was only a prayer for the bishops of the Church and no mention of the pope…because there is no pope. Also at the time of the prayers for the dead, the priest prayed "for our brother John Paul…in baptism he died with Christ, may he also share his resurrection." That moment made things hit home for me.

It has been an exhausting two days, to say the least. Tomorrow morning, Sunday morning, there will be a Mass celebrated in St. Peter's Square at 10:30 AM. I hope to attend and to continue to be a privileged witness to these momentous days.

Years and years from now, we will all be telling the story of these days. For each person I know there is a specific gift and message from God during this graced time. I know because I am witnessing an outpouring of grace in this city of the apostles Peter and Paul.

"Do not be afraid! Open wide the doors to Christ!" These were the words of the pope as he opened his pontificate more than twenty-six years ago. Tonight, as his pontificate ended, Christ opened wide the doors to John Paul II. May God grant him eternal rest.

The unprecedented outpouring of emotion at the passing of the Holy Father was in large part due to the way he reached out to all the people of the world, especially young people. Beginning in 1985 in Argentina, Pope John Paul II met regularly with them at what became known as World Youth Day, and literally millions of young Catholics today can trace the beginning of their journey of faith to one of these powerful and joyful encounters. A few of them share their stories here.

One-Way Ticket

Chris Amateis, Nebraska

I walked onto the long charter bus full of bubbly college students. We were bound for a journey from which I have never truly returned.

I'd been living the party life since high school. I didn't care about anything or anyone, and it showed. It wasn't the life I wanted to live, but I was buried in sin on top of sin, without any direction. At that point I didn't even give a thought to the sacraments. I was desperate for God, but I had no idea how to find him on my own. I entered the bus that day completely on a whim.

At that point, I had been attending Sunday Mass superstitiously—I thought it made my weeks go better—and I actually got pretty excited when the priest at the parish told the congregation that Pope John Paul II was coming to North America and would be at this "World Youth Day" thing. I called my mom right away with excitement and said, "The pope is coming!" My family had a humble financial background, so I was a little shocked when she said, "You're going no matter what it takes."

Her words resonated with me as I took my seat on the bus. The doors shut, the wheels began rolling and I settled in for the thirty-hour trip to Toronto, Canada.

There is nothing like World Youth Day. Nowhere else on earth will you find a bigger gathering of truly Christ-centered love and enthusiasm. The event seems to be infused with a kind of electricity that literally could light up the world. So it was no mere coincidence that the 2002 WYD slogan was, "You are the salt of the earth; you are the light of the world."

It was an amazing week of nothing but joyful feelings from every person you looked at, spoke to, listened to, sang with, ate with (and even smelled at times) in the crowded atmosphere, and spending the last two days with John Paul II was like winning the Heavenly Super Bowl! The ongoing festivities were transforming the cold hole in my heart, but the most inspiring thing was just being in the same environment with John Paul II. When the popemobile parted the crowds, my hardened heart began to feel a renewed excitement and I shed some long-coming tears.

At the all-night vigil John Paul didn't sit next to the huge altar as just a pope. Even with his ailing health, he was our compassionate father, sent to us by God to convey his loving message of faith, hope and love. His wonderful words rang true, they made sense and they shook me to my core. The pope's love was returned—when he stated his age, thousands of voices repeatedly rang out, "The pope is young!" His smile was unforgettable. He brought us together as a Christian family, and everyone there felt like brothers and sisters.

The most memorable moment for me occurred at dusk. The pope lit a candle. From his candle more were lit, then more from those, and more and more, until the whole world around us was shining with brilliance. It was only a matter of minutes before mine was lit—a light that lit the night with the fire of Jesus' love for us, manifested through John Paul II. If we felt like family before, it was confirmed with the proof that we all were one big light of Jesus Christ to the entire world. The tears, joy and love that poured from us made us into one body and the salt of the earth.

I began to consider myself a part of the generation called by God through John Paul II to become something greater. As we headed back home, I made a crucial decision to go to confession and start my life over. Absolution cleansed my soul, and the life I had led before WYD was washed away. I was transformed by something I didn't ever plan to encounter: Jesus' love for me.

I could never go back to whom I had been in the past, so I stretched out my new legs and have been running the race ever since. I've fallen more times than I would like to admit, but the sacraments sustain me. Pope John Paul II truly made a difference in my life.

Trust God Because He Trusts You
Kaeleigh Abbott, Nebraska

Pope John Paul II is my hero. Through his encyclicals and his amazing accomplishments, and also through my visits with him, I have received encouragement, inspiration and guidance. During his life he displayed the strength and humility I long to emulate. He is the example that I look to, the person who has been for me a witness of Christ.

Throughout my Catholic education I was repeatedly drilled about the importance of the sacraments, Mary, the saints and the rosary. However, my prayer life was weak, and I never felt a personal urge to truly and fully be a Catholic. I wanted to understand the connection between my life and God.

I was sixteen years old when I went to Toronto, Canada, where the pope drew youth from all over the globe for World Youth Day 2002. At WYD I discovered that there is no language barrier with Christ. While I was there, I came to realize that we are all truly one family in faith. Solidarity enveloped us as we grew closer to Christ. We "invaded" Canada, and the Canadians reached out to us as brothers and sisters in Christ. Our world, then as now, was torn with violence and hatred, but Pope John Paul II welcomed every one of us in peace and in the name of Christ.

My WYD pilgrimage progressed as if the Holy Spirit was guiding me along—as if I was there for something in particular—making sure I saw his message.

We visited beautiful churches, historical places and people from around the world. We joined together for Holy Mass and listened to many speakers. We waited in anticipation with one hope—we wanted to see and hear Pope John Paul II speak to us. For most of us this was the only pope we had ever known. Finally the day arrived. Enormous crowds of eager youth awaited his arrival. I remember seeing the three helicopters fly overhead and my heart began to race. He came through the crowds in the popemobile. Tears raced down my cheeks, and I trembled inside and out. Seeing the pope was the most powerful feeling I had ever experienced. The Holy Spirit's presence enveloped me, and I felt as if I was seeing Christ drive right in front of me.

The pope was speaking to thousands of youth that day, but I felt as if he was speaking directly to me when he said, "Trust God because he trusts you." After hearing the pope speak that day, I had so much hope. He encouraged all of us to be witnesses to Christ. He inspired me and deepened my love of Christ, which in turn has shaped the relationships I have with those who surround me today. The strength I gained has affected my fallen-away family and improved the meaning of my friendships.

At the closing Mass the pope again told us that we needed to be strong for Christ. I left Canada that day with my heart on fire and my faith relit with an unquenchable passion.

From that day on I have never stopped yearning for Mass, and I find myself yearning for the consecration of the Eucharist and Holy Communion even more. I want to do everything possible to follow in the pope's footsteps to be all I can be for Jesus.

During the summer of 2003, just two weeks before my friends left for Rome on a pilgrimage, I felt urged to join them. Once again the Holy Spirit was directing my actions. I was driven by the ongoing desire to learn as much as I could about my faith and to see John Paul again.

We were blessed to attend his weekly audience. The same feeling came over me that I felt in Toronto as he passed. I remember thinking, "He is an amazing witness to Christ. I long for the closeness he has with Jesus and our Mother Mary."

I was blessed to have been in the presence of Pope John Paul II twice. My faith before those occasions was mediocre and weak, and I struggled to have fire in my heart for Christ. But my faith was renewed by the message of Pope John Paul II. I now find my fire for Christ hard to contain.

I experienced the great love that the pope had for the youth. In return, I love him. With hundreds of thousands of others from nations around the world, I chanted, "John Paul II, we love you!" He told me to trust in God. From that moment on, my faith has been my greatest possession. He taught me to cling to Christ in times of suffering and joy. The moments I have spent praying and listening to John Paul speak are now my foundation to endure all the trials that life may bring.

May John Paul the Great rest in peace, and may he remain in the hearts and minds of all of us.

The Saints of the New Millennium
Leah Bethune, England

We had anticipated this great moment for almost a year. Now we stood among millions of other young people, priests, parents and friends inside of St. Peter's Square, brought together for World Youth Day 2000. We arrived in the Square early, so we would be able to get a good view of the popemobile as it passed. However, by the time we arrived, thousands of people with the same idea had already arrived. I could feel my emotions begin to get unpredictable. One minute I was so overjoyed and excited, and the next I was a little discouraged, thinking, "This moment is never really going to come," and, "I am unworthy of what is about to happen." We pushed and pulled our way through hundreds of people to get up to the rope lining the path of the popemobile. Just as we arrived, we heard people beginning to cheer. The moment had come.

As we got out our cameras, I started to cry. I felt so happy and yet so unworthy. A few of us students began to hold hands and pray. Just then he drove past. We yelled, held up our hands in hopes that he would reach in our direction and took pictures of him. An amazing feeling of peace came over me as he passed. I went from being on an emotional roller coaster to being completely at peace. I felt worthy to be there in his sight; I felt as if he wanted me there. Some of my friends were experiencing the same thing, and we all knelt down and said a few prayers together as we waited to hear him speak to us.

We knew that we were not going to understand what he was saying because he was going to speak in Italian and Latin, so we gathered around a radio to listen to the translation. He greeted us all with words of welcome and excitement. Then he said the words that forever changed my life, "Young people of every continent, do not be afraid to become the saints of the new millennium!" He went on to tell us how important we were to the Catholic Church and how it needed us. He spoke about how we needed to step up and listen to the call of God. He told us that God had a plan for our lives and it was a special plan. God was going to use us to make his Church grow stronger. The pope also told us that we had faith stronger than many he had seen and that our faith would lead us. His words made so much sense to me. He was right.

I thought our Church was struggling, but sitting there looking at all of those young people who had such a strong faith and cared enough to travel to WYD, I felt as if our Church had nothing to worry about. *We* are the Church, and we are the future. I left the square that day feeling as if I were on top of the world, because I knew that along with all of these young people I was going to improve the Church. I knew I was an important part of the Church and that *I mattered* to the pope.

I heard the pope speak one other time during WYD, and he conveyed the same message to us. The more I thought about and prayed about his words, I began to realize that I was going to have to lead my life differently, because if the pope believed in me then I could believe in myself. I went from being an ordinary high school graduate to a person who believed in the purpose of Christ and believed that I had a part in it. I began evaluating my life and the way I was living it. I wanted to be a saint, and I knew that there were things in my life that weren't going in that direction. I started going to Mass more, praying more and really trying to get a message out of everything, because I knew that God was calling me to something.

A few years passed as I continued in my search; I began discerning my vocation. Then one day I came across some notes I had made about the pope's speech, and I realized that Christ was calling me to educate youth about their importance in the Church. So I began working as a youth minister at church, giving presentations at national conferences and heading youth retreats to explain the message I'd found so important to my life. The pope was not talking only to me that day in Rome but to millions of youth around the world. I know that the influence Pope John Paul II had on me is one that will live forever, not only in my own life but also in the lives of thousands of teens with whom I have interacted during the during the past few years and those with whom I will interact in years to come. Pope John Paul II changed the way I live my life, and I struggle every day to be the saint he has called me to become.

CHAPTER THREE

Divine Mercy Outpoured

Mankind will not have peace until it turns with trust to My mercy.

—Sister Faustina Kowalska, *Diary*[1]

Sunday, April 3, 2005—ROME

Give thanks to the LORD, for he is good, for his mercy endures forever" (Psalm 136:1).

As this Divine Mercy Sunday comes to a close, the words of the psalm response in today's Mass are a fitting way to express the cascade of emotions which have filled the hearts of everyone in the Eternal City on this day unlike any my generation has ever known—a day on which there was no pope. We are filled with sadness, yet at the same time how can we fail to thank God for the abundant gift of his mercy given to the Church and to the whole world in the person and pontificate of John Paul the Great? This day has been another panoply of images, indelible moments and personal encounters leaving their mark on the soul. Here is how Rome spent the Feast of Divine Mercy 2005.

Pope John Paul instituted the Feast of Divine Mercy for the Church during the Great Jubilee of the Year 2000, to be held each year on the Sunday after Easter, in accord with the locutions of Jesus recorded by Saint Faustina Kowalska in her diary entitled *Divine Mercy in My Soul.* It was ten years ago today, on Divine Mercy Sunday 1995, that John Paul dedicated the Divine Mercy shrine for the city of Rome. He chose to place it in the seventeenth-century Church of the Holy Spirit, just one block from the Vatican on the Borgo Santo Spirito near the Tiber River, a prominent spot in view of the dome of St. Peter's Basilica. To mark this anniversary, a Mass had been scheduled weeks ago to be celebrated by a Polish bishop. I concelebrated that Mass at 9:30 this morning, which was attended by dozens of priests and over 2,000 people who packed themselves into the relatively small church and overflowed into the piazza outside. The scene reminded me of the story in the second chapter of the Gospel of Saint Mark, when there were so many people in the house that the paralytic had to be lowered down through the roof. Picture a church in which every pew is squeezed full, every aisle is full of people sitting on the floor, every side chapel has people standing all but on top of each other, and all the entrances are blocked. One could have said it was standing room only, except for the fact that there was no standing room!

Holy cards were distributed that had been printed long in advance, with the date April 3, 2005, and the quotation, "*Siate apostoli della Divina Misericordia!*"— "Be apostles of Divine Mercy!"—the words of Pope John Paul when he blessed the shrine at this church on Divine Mercy Sunday, 1995. The Polish bishop who celebrated the Mass this morning (whose name escapes me and at any rate is very difficult to spell!) preached in Italian about the way in which Pope John Paul lived his mission of announcing Divine Mercy to the world. At one point he thundered from the pulpit, "Pope John Paul will be remembered in history as the Pope of Divine Mercy!" and the entire church thundered back in applause.

At Communion time I literally climbed over people and made my way down what appeared to be an aisle to give Communion. The people *could not move* due to the crowd. So I made my way around, constantly being tapped, pulled and begged to bring Communion here or there. It was such a consolation to be able to bring the Eucharist to the people on this feast. As I did so, I was thinking, "Even though the pope is dead, we still have Christ with us! The Church goes on! The sacraments do not cease!" Certainly we give thanks to the Lord for the merciful gift of his Church, which may be lacking a visible head but remains eternally united to her invisible Head who is Jesus Christ.

After Mass I remained at the shrine altar of the Divine Mercy image showing the two rays of blood and water streaming from Christ's wounded side. I stood there distributing Communion to those who had been unable to receive during the Mass—this lasted for a good twenty minutes after Mass had ended.

In the sacristy after Mass I asked the Polish nuns if there was any English Mass scheduled in the church during the day. When they told me no, I offered to say one. They agreed to have an English Mass at 5:00 PM. Saint Faustina must have been working overtime on that one, because at first they had told me there was no possibility, but then said they could fit me in between a Polish Mass at 4:00 and an Italian Mass at 6:00. More on that Mass later.

I walked the short distance to St. Peter's Square where the first memorial Mass for the pope was just reaching Holy Communion (it was about 11:30 AM). This scene was by far the most powerful one yet. I will try to explain:

The square was once again jammed with tens of thousands of people, extending far beyond the piazza and down to the river. The celebrant of the Mass was Cardinal Angelo Sodano, who was Secretary of State under John Paul II (all cardinals lose their particular offices as secretaries or prefects upon the death of the pope, as their only duty is now to run the Church until the election of the new pope). Two particular details of the scene immediately struck me and shook me:

First, the red canopy, which always stands over the

altar when a Mass is celebrated in the square, was gone. There was a simple altar and crucifix sitting in the middle of the stone pavement in front of the basilica at which Cardinal Sodano offered Mass. It looked so bare.

Second, the fourth window over from the right on the top floor of the papal apartments was standing open. Normally on Sunday mornings the second window from the right is opened and the familiar red drape hangs out of it so that the pope can speak to the crowds. But that window was closed. The fourth window was open, with nothing hanging under it, and from the square below all one could see inside the window was blackness. This window marked the Sala Clementina, where the pope's body was lying in state, waiting to be viewed by the cardinals after the Mass. The stark and hollow emptiness of that black window is an image I shall never forget. It was something like seeing the empty tabernacle standing open on Good Friday. The altar has been stripped and the Vicar of Christ has been taken away.

I made my way slowly through the crowd as hymns were sung and Communion was being distributed in the front of the piazza, probably only to a few thousand people, a mere fraction of the number of people in the square. The obelisk of Nero towered above the crowd. This obelisk was one of the last things seen by Saint Peter before his crucifixion in the Circus of Nero, on the site of the present St. Peter's Square and Basilica, in AD 64. That obelisk witnessed the death of the first pope, and now, 1,941 years later, it is witnessing the death of the 265th pope. Such is the depth of the history and tradition of the Catholic Church.

I felt a desire to get up above the crowd, and so I hopped up onto a lamppost to the left of the obelisk. For about ten minutes I perched on the ledge supporting the lamp. It all started hitting me as I gazed around at the crowd, the bare altar, the black window, the dome of the basilica, the cardinals, the empty white chair by the altar, the mass of cameras and microphones lining the edge of the square. I started whispering, "Lord, have mercy on us," praying for all this mass of humanity gathered here and fixing their eyes on this place from all over the world. It became clear to me that we were witnessing salvation history. This was a milestone, and the Church and the world will never be the same again after the pontificate of John Paul II. This moment of his passing was undoubtedly a moment of conversion for countless souls, a moment of opening to grace, which will never be repeated.

I was called out of my meditation by two Italian security guards who tugged at my leg and insisted I come down. I looked down at them and said in the most distraught voice, "*Ma non capite? Il Papa e morto!*" (But don't you understand? The pope is dead!). They looked at me, a little taken aback. I apologized and came down and walked away. I felt like I was six years old and my world had been taken away from me, and nobody could possibly understand.

I walked closer to the front of the piazza and then stopped to hear the reading of the Regina Coeli address. (This prayer is said at noontime during the Easter season in place of the Angelus. The pope had always given this address and prayer from his window at noon on Sundays.) The archbishop who read it announced that what he was about to read was being read at the explicit instructions of Pope John Paul. He began, "Today we celebrate the Feast of Divine Mercy…". I realized in that moment that the pope had known exactly when he was going to be taken from us and had prepared everything just for this moment. The words seemed to come from the heavens. I really broke down then—the pope *knew*; he foresaw this moment and left words to comfort us, his lost, orphaned children; he was still speaking to us from beyond the veil…. I don't remember much of the rest of the message. I think you could have collected a few glasses of my tears.

We prayed the Regina Coeli, and Cardinal Sodano gave the blessing. I looked up at the windows and remembered looking up at those same windows exactly a week ago during the Regina Coeli on Easter, seeing the pope standing and struggling and blessing us in silence. But he did not come to the window today. I kept waiting for him to appear. Maybe the last few days all really were a strange dream. But no, he will never stand at his window again, nor will we ever hear his voice resound-through the square giving the blessing in Latin, "*Benedicat vos omnipotens Deus…*".

I went toward the back of the square, sat on the ground near some students, and prayed the Liturgy of the Hours (the psalms and Scripture readings that all priests and religious, as well as many laypeople, pray each day). The black, open window kept drawing my eyes. It captured the finality and emptiness of this day.

I started back to my residence for lunch with my brother priests, many of whom had concelebrated the Mass in the square (I had given my allegiance to Saint Faustina and had gone to her church for the earlier Mass). As I made my way down the Via della Conciliazione toward the Tiber, I saw hundreds of people gathered in front of two JumboTron screens on either side of the street, all jostling for a view and cran-ing their necks. When I got to a point where I could see what they were all looking at, I saw the cardinal *camer-lengo* (chamberlain) in the Vatican apartments sprin-kling holy water on the body of the pope, which was laid out in red Mass vestments, which are always placed on the remains of a deceased pontiff. The picture was just fuzzy enough that I thought it was an old news clip of

Paul VI or John Paul I being laid in state. I asked a man next to me, "Is that from an old news story?" His answer, "This is live from the Vatican apartments" again was a moment that made things hit home. I took a deep breath and again shook my head in disbelief as I looked on the body of John Paul II. I saw a close-up later and noticed that the right side of the face was quite bruised and swollen. He must have suffered much in his final days and hours.

Lunch at our house consisted of exchanging stories of the last twenty-four hours. Where were you when you heard the news? Did you see this? Did you hear that? When will the funeral be? When will the conclave open? And of course, being a house of priests, everyone has his or her strong opinion and prediction about who the next pope will be!

After lunch I had thought of stealing a quick nap, but I ended up reading Italian newspaper coverage and then going online for a bit to read up on the latest and see what everyone is saying (even in Rome we are getting the latest from the Internet). There is too much going on around here to think of sleep. My eyes do not like me very much right now.

At 5:00 PM I celebrated Mass in English back at the shrine of the Divine Mercy. The church was mobbed, slightly down from the unbelievable crowd of the morning, meaning this time there was *some* standing room. I preached on the connection between Saint Faustina and

John Paul the Great. Two points that I made to the young people gathered there and to all who came follow:

> First, this day of mourning for the pope should have happened on May 14, 1981, the day after the assassination attempt in which John Paul should have died. The fact that he did not and that he reigned for nearly twenty-four more years is a miracle of grace given to the world by the direct intervention of Our Lady of Fatima, on whose feast day the pope was shot. Had he died in 1981, none of the young people at the Mass, many of them under twenty years old, would ever have known him. This means that every day of his pontificate since May 13, 1981, has been a gift to the world from God through the Blessed Mother's intercession and protection. "Give thanks to the Lord for he is good, his mercy endures forever!"
>
> Second, in the novena of preparation for the Feast of Divine Mercy (recorded by Saint Faustina in her diary), Jesus asks that nine days of prayer will precede the Feast of Divine Mercy, beginning on Good Friday, and on each day he asks for prayers for particular souls. On the seventh day Jesus asks, "Today bring to me the souls who especially venerate and glorify My mercy."[2] It struck me that this seventh day was Thursday, March 31, the day on which the pope entered his death struggle…the Lord called John Paul to himself, bringing close to him his servant who more than any other has venerated and glorified his Divine Mercy. Christ's promise in the *Diary* is that "I shall particularly defend each one of them at the hour of death."[3] Was this not seen in the thousands of souls who

came to pray in St. Peter's Square during the vigil of the pope's suffering and death, who accompanied him on the Way of the Cross by their prayers and love? Jesus promises Faustina, "These souls will shine with a special brightness in the next life."[4] I think we are only beginning to glimpse the greatness of the splendor of this new saint. The Church awoke today in sadness without a pope, but it awoke in joy, a joy that I know will only increase as we begin to appreciate and fathom the greatness and depth and powerful spiritual presence of our new intercessor, John Paul the Great.

Historically, on the day after the death of a pope the Church celebrates a Requiem Mass, wearing colors of mourning and praying the prayers of the dead. John Paul, ever one to break with protocol, has done something different. His death on the vigil of the feast *he* instituted meant that the Church had no choice this morning but to awake, put on the golden vestments of the Resurrection and celebrate the octave of Easter, Divine Mercy Sunday, singing, "Gloria in Excelsis Deo," and dismissing the faithful at Mass with a double Alleluia.

John Paul began Divine Mercy Sunday with Mass and viaticum in the papal apartments. He is ending it in the company of the Risen Lord, Our Lady of Fatima, and Saint Faustina. How could the Church not celebrate, even as it mourns? It is liturgically a day of unbridled joy in the resurrection of Jesus Christ who is mercy incarnate. And that is exactly the way John Paul the Great wants it to be.

"Give thanks to the LORD, for he is good, for his mercy endures forever."

One of the ways in which Pope John Paul II revolutionized the Church's understanding of holiness was by his fervent teaching on the dignity and holiness of marriage and the family. His "Theology of the Body" joyfully proclaims the power of married love to draw husbands, wives and their children into the communion of life and love that is the Holy Trinity. Several married couples now share the profound gift they were privileged to receive together through encountering John Paul II.

The Greatest Blessing of Our Marriage

Scott and Sarah Aurit, Nebraska

Beginning when we were college students, John Paul II has had a great impact on our lives. Through his teachings, he helped bring us closer to the Church and deepened our understanding of our call to the vocation of marriage. We were married on July 14, 2001, and decided to take a delayed honeymoon to Rome to have our marriage blessed. We were inspired by the pope's invitation for newly married couples to travel to Rome to receive his personal blessing.

We had the trip all planned—and then the tragic events of September 11, 2001, occurred. Travel advisories were issued, cautioning Americans overseas and especially those in Italy. Our parents strongly encouraged us to forgo our plans. Then in November 2001, our new life together was blessed when we found out that

Sarah was pregnant. This caused further concern from our families about the safety of travel.

After much prayer, we decided to persevere with the trip. We felt that this was a once-in-a-lifetime opportunity. We prayed for an uneventful journey, particularly when, just days before our departure, another threat of terrorism caused panic. On our way to the airport, we specifically prayed for a priest to be on our flight in the event that we would need a last-minute general absolution. That prayer was answered when *four* priests boarded our plane! One of them sat directly in front of us during the flight.

After arriving in Rome, we couldn't wait for the opportunity to see the Holy Father. We first saw John Paul II during the Te Deum celebration on the evening of December 31, 2001, and also during Mass celebrating the Solemnity of Mary the Mother of God on January 1, 2002. These two experiences with the Holy Father were a small precursor to the actual event of receiving his blessing for our marriage during his weekly audience.

Sarah had packed her wedding dress and was thankful that her pregnancy had not yet progressed to a point that she couldn't wear it. We put on our wedding clothes and walked the three blocks from our hotel to the Paul VI Audience Hall—to the enthusiastic cheers of Italians on the street. Anticipation continued to build as we were seated with thirty newlywed couples from around the world. The pope's love for marriage and family life was far-reaching and universal.

We couldn't get a clear view of John Paul as we made our way up the marble stairs to where he was seated. As the couple in front of us walked away after receiving their blessing, we were astonished to see the Holy Father looking directly at us. We were overcome with emotion, and could feel the presence of immense grace radiating from him. The effects of time and his Parkinson's disease were apparent, but it seemed only to make his spiritual strength greater. As we leaned forward to speak with him, Sarah began to cry. The pope reached out his hand to touch her cheek and gently wipe away the tear. He gave us his blessing and wished us a happy new year. We replied, "We love you and are praying for you." It was a moment we will never forget.

His blessing has created a profound effect on our family that will last generations. Our son was born on August 17, 2002. We named him John Paul. Though he was only in his earliest weeks of life, we know that being in the Holy Father's presence changed his life.

The Holy Father's passing in April, 2005, was very difficult for us and we found it hard to comprehend that he had actually gone away. He was the only pope we had ever known. Although he has now left this world, we know that he is now truly closer to us.

His writings continue to teach us. Sarah now teaches Natural Family Planning, and we have dedicated ourselves to working with engaged couples planning for marriage, emphasizing the "Theology of the Body" teachings of John Paul II. He has taught us how to live the words, "Be not afraid," and to embrace our sufferings. We believe that the influence of John Paul II is only just beginning in our lives; it will take many years for us to fully comprehend how strong his blessing truly is on our marriage and our family.

Our Spiritual "Papa"

Chris and Anne Lautenschlager, Nebraska

As the pope made his dramatic entrance to the welcoming ceremony at World Youth Day 2002 in Toronto, we could tell the Holy Father was completely energized by all of us young people around him. We sang joyfully, and as he sat in his chair, he tapped his hand on the table in front of him in time with the music.

Even though we were many yards away from the Holy Father, it seemed that he was speaking specifically to us, as a father would speak to his children. He praised our commitment to the Church, but at the same time he urged us to do more: to be the salt of the earth, adding flavor to life, and to be light to the world, to shine for everyone around us. When he came through the crowds in the popemobile, he had such a peaceful and happy face.

The following year, after answering God's call to the vocation of marriage, we traveled to Rome to receive the special marriage blessing the pope gives to newlyweds at his weekly audience. Though his body was suffering, when we looked into his eyes, an indescribable peace swept over us. He was just *radiating* peace. We knelt before him, and even though he had been sitting there with thousands of people in front of him, he looked at us as if we were the only people who had come to meet him that day. As he raised his hand to bless us, it was really the culmination of God's call for us to the vocation of marriage. Pope John Paul II understood the beauty of each individual vocation, and now that we had embraced ours, he was like our father, happy that we had answered God's call, wanting us to go forth and live a life of holiness in our vocation.

We could tell it was painful for him just to keep raising his hand to bless those coming to him, but he denied his body in order to serve others as the long lines of people kept streaming toward him. As he was welcoming all those gathered, periodically applause and shouts would interrupt him, and although he was so tired, he would carefully lift his head and look out to acknowledge those in the audience. More than any words he spoke, he was giving us a living example of sacrifice.

His blessing has empowered us to continue to live out our faith and build up God's kingdom within our own family and our vocation to marriage. We call upon that blessing often, asking that the graces we received from God through the Holy Father will be applied to whatever hardships or struggles we face, or simply that these graces will help us better live out our vocation as a married couple.

Being in the presence of Pope John Paul II fueled in us a great desire for holiness. Pope John Paul II believed in us young people as the future of the Church and the world. He called us to discover our calling from God and to live out our faith in whatever vocation we were given. He will probably always be the most influential of our spiritual "papas."

Fearless Families

Tony and Cyndi Ojeda, Nebraska

August, 1993, found us as two young people engaged to be married. We came to World Youth Day in Denver as part of a youth outreach group to evangelize other young people through talks, music and skits. We were in the springtime of our love for each other and of our faith. Tony had recommitted to his faith with the kind of zeal and passion that would be the hallmark of the JPII generation. Cyndi had found the home she had looked for all her life. Having just been baptized and received into the Church at Easter that year, she waited as a "baby Catholic" to see her Papa.

Our group had tickets to all the events but never enough for all of us to go to the same event. Because of this, Cyndi and one other girl were allowed—after much pleading, praying and tears—to have the two tickets we were allotted for the papal welcome at Mile High Stadium. The memories of the many helicopters flying over, not knowing which one held our long-awaited Holy Father, are still vivid and fresh. When the moment came and His Holiness came onto the stage, all Cyndi had to give was her heart. No more words were left, just tears. She knew the Church was her family and this was her Papa. She wished she could share this moment with Tony, but he had sacrificed to let her go as he stayed behind to finish up their work. He knew he would have an opportunity to see the pope at the Vigil and Mass. When that time came, Tony found that he too was speechless. Surrounded by his brothers and sisters in faith from all over the world, Tony became acutely aware of the universality of the Church for the first time.

Together at the vigil, Tony and Cyndi sat with a half-million young people and listened to the words and wisdom of John Paul II. "Everything in you—your mind and heart, will and freedom, gifts and talents—everything is being taken up by the Holy Spirit in order to make you 'living stones' of the 'spiritual house' which is the Church (cf. 1 Peter 2:5)."[5] It was overwhelming to be in his presence, and together we shared in a true and deeply spiritual joy.

Waking the next morning on the cold ground that was covered with pilgrims, we prepared for Mass. Tony prayed with a renewed fervor for God's will to be done in his life, and Cyndi prayed with much thanksgiving for being Catholic. The Holy Father's words in his homily—words that still resonate with us to this day—solidified how we as a couple would strive to live out our married life. "The Church needs your energies, your enthusiasm, your youthful ideals, in order to make the Gospel of Life penetrate the fabric of society."[6] Throughout our years of married life this has been our goal.

November, 2004, found us married for ten years and making another pilgrimage, this time to Rome to be with our "Papa" for what we felt would be one last time. We started the day by walking from the prison where Saints Peter and Paul spent their last days, continuing through the Roman Forum, past the Colosseum and down the Appian Way. Retracing their route enkindled in our hearts a deep appreciation for the sacrifice the martyrs made, a sacrifice that resulted in the growth of the holy mother Church. Going down into the catacombs and having Mass with our dearest friends was a great privilege. We felt that the communion of saints had become tangible.

The day was crowned with the moment for which we had come to the Eternal City, a chance to see our beloved Holy Father at Mass at the Vatican. It had been a last-minute decision for the pope to attend due to his frailty. We were able to find spots right on the aisle and waited, our anticipation magnified by the day's events. The Swiss Guards processed up the main aisle, and everyone present knew who would be following them. As the Holy Father was moved through the center of St. Peter's Basilica, emotion took over the crowd. Tears were mixed with prayers for this man. Though we knew him to be tired, frail and ill, we knew that he still had the same interior desire to be with us as he did in Denver. Much of what he said that night was lost, not because of translation but because of the profound movement of the heart that we experienced.

Here before us was the reality of martyrdom, the Lord's suffering servant. This moment inspired us in our marriage and in our commitment to living out our vocation with this same vision of sacrificial love: love for our children, love for the Church and love for her faithful people. John Paul II had called us to embrace the cross in our vocation as a family: "Dear families, you too should be fearless, ever ready to give witness to the hope that is in you (cf. 1 Pet 3:15).... You should be ready to follow Christ towards the pastures of life, which he himself has prepared through the Paschal Mystery of his Death and Resurrection."[7]

We wanted to take all that our Papa had taught us and was now physically living and embrace it with all our hearts. When he died a few months later, we were left with gratitude and love for these images of our Papa.

Preach From the Rooftops
Jenny Lugardo, Illinois

World Youth Day 1993 in Denver is long past, but I can still hear John Paul II in Cherry Creek Park saying, "This is no time to be ashamed of the gospel. It is time to preach it from the rooftops."[8] He encouraged the young people present to imitate the early apostles in their fearless preaching of the gospel. Those words stayed with me through adolescence, and I tried hard to live that message among my friends in high school, even picking up the nickname "pope" because I was such a big John Paul II fan.

After high school I worked for a year before heading to college. That year I read some of the pope's plays. I came to recognize the Holy Father's love of family life, and through his writing I began to see the great holiness of the home.

My college years provided a big "rooftop." Through pro-life activism I had many opportunities to preach the gospel of life, and the Holy Father's words from WYD provided encouragement. The words with which the Holy Father opened his pontificate and constantly repeated—"Do not be afraid!"—also resounded in my heart.

I continued reading the writings of the Holy Father and plowed through part of his *Theology of the Body*. During this time I was attempting to discern my vocation, and I found the writings of John Paul II to be very helpful. Through his words, I realized how perfectly each person's vocation matches his or her personhood. I finally understood that discernment did not mean figuring out some cosmic plan; it meant figuring out the glory for which God had specifically created me.

I had always been attracted to the holiness and charity of women religious, but in reading the Holy Father's writings, I became convinced that the domestic Church also possesses tremendous sanctity. This was the path God laid in front of me.

During the Great Jubilee of the Year 2000, I once again went to World Youth Day. There in Rome the pope called us to be the "saints of the new millennium." He said it with such hope that we would respond generously. He seemed convinced that all two million of us could become saints, and I did not want to disappoint him.

In 2002 I went to World Youth Day in Toronto with my brother and some close friends, including my boyfriend who is now my husband. Seeing the pope both in Toronto and later that summer in Rome taught me a very important lesson that I needed to learn before getting married. The pope's voice was weak and his movements were difficult, but his presence was strong because it was full of love. The idea of "preaching from the rooftops" had been with me for so long, and I was struggling to understand how I could continue to do that as a wife and mother. The Holy Father's example showed me that the gospel can be preached loudly, without words, simply by loving at all times, in all places.

My husband and I both found a mentor in John Paul II, and guided by his words and the teaching of the holy mother Church we entered marriage with a complete openness to life, knowing that for us it would mean poverty and sacrifice. When I became pregnant with our son, I was too sick to work. Not being able to leave the couch, I had lots of time to read the pope's official biography, *Witness to Hope*, by George Weigel (New York: HarperCollins, 1999). It was inspiring and touching—the tenderest part for me was reading about the families that were the Holy Father's dear friends in Poland and how he guided them. Though separated by many years and miles, I felt like my little family was one of them.

These days my rooftop is a sink full of dirty dishes or a grocery store line, and I think the Holy Father would approve.

CHAPTER FOUR

The Procession

*Christ will lead us more deeply into the Church,
his Body and his Bride. In this way we see how
rich in meaning are the words of the Apostle Peter
when he writes that, united to Christ, we too are
built, like living stones, "into a spiritual house, to
be a holy priesthood, to offer spiritual sacrifices
acceptable to God" (1 Pt 2:5).*

—John Paul II, *Incarnationis Mysterium*[1]

Monday, April 4, 2005—ROME

It is impossible to describe the conditions in this city. As I write, helicopters are hovering overhead, traffic is backed up down the entire Corso Vittorio Emmanuele leading through the heart of the city toward the Vatican, and it is said that up to six hundred thousand people are in line to view the body of John Paul II, with well over a *million* having already viewed it. I have just returned from the Via della Conciliazione, which runs from St. Peter's Square to the Tiber, and witnessed the unbelievable sight of three different lines converging,

57

each one containing tens of thousands of people. Two of the lines go over the bridge, across the river and then along the banks of the Tiber as far as the eye can see. Water bottles are stacked up by the side of the road by the thousands and are being distributed in a very disorganized way in the hot afternoon sun. The line moves in stages and is now said to be over twelve hours long. All this to walk past the Holy Father's body for a few seconds at the most. I was in the basilica at noon today for a memorial Mass offered for the pope and was deeply moved by the devotion and prayerfulness of the pilgrims who were coming into St. Peter's. Their exhaustion was also evident; as I prayed at the side altar of Saint Gregory the Great, dozens of people came and collapsed on the steps near the altar after hours in the line.

Last night, as I left the area around St. Peter's Square around midnight, I hopped on a bus heading away from the Vatican toward the main train station, Roma Termini. As we went away from St. Peter's we passed a bus about every twenty to thirty yards, each one *jammed* full of pilgrims. I counted nearly forty buses going the other way during my five-minute bus ride home. Mind you, this was at midnight! People are arriving at Termini station, immediately getting on a bus, and getting in the enormous line to view the pope's body *with their luggage*. Many people are wheeling bags behind them as they make the twelve-hour march. Suffice it to say that we are witnessing something totally unprecedented in history. Yes, there have been countless papal funerals before, but this is going far beyond even a papal funeral and becoming a historical event of unequalled magnitude. An older priest I heard from today said that there is absolutely no way to compare what is transpiring with the funerals of either John XXIII or Paul VI. John Paul II, the actor, has in death taken the world stage in a way even he himself may not have foreseen.

This morning and again this evening a memorial Mass was held at the "Altar of the Chair," created by Bernini in the sixteenth century and located at the very back of the basilica beneath the famous "Holy Spirit window." It was standing room only in the enormous sanctuary at 10:30 AM as approximately four hundred priests with five bishops concelebrated Mass for the repose of the Holy Father's soul. The Italian bishop who preached gave a powerful and spirit-filled exhortation to imitate the Holy Father's forgiveness of others in our daily lives, citing the example of John Paul forgiving Ali Agca, his would-be assassin, and meeting with him in his prison cell in 1982. (I heard today that Ali Agca petitioned the Turkish government to be allowed to attend the funeral but was refused because he is still serving his prison sentence.)

I must say that while simply being in Rome at this time is overwhelming, the added unspeakable privilege of being a priest in Rome right now goes beyond my capacity to express. This fact has not been lost on me.

This morning my brother priests and I were able to walk into a back entrance to St. Peter's Basilica, vest in the sacristy and process out past the pope's body to celebrate Mass, while thousands of others waited all night to get in the church for a few minutes at most. Several of us talked on the way in about the extraordinary privilege we are being given and the corresponding responsibility we have to share with others for the rest of our lives what we are witnessing (one of the main reasons I am writing!).

Now I must tell the story of what for me was the most extraordinary moment thus far in a week of extraordinary moments, the transfer of the pope's body from the Apostolic Palace to St. Peter's Basilica. On Monday afternoon, April 4, I had just returned home from lunch and thought I was going to have a few minutes for a much-needed nap, when a quick knock came on the door of my room, and two of the priests who lived with me told me that the rumor was out that all priests were invited to take part in the procession accompanying the pope's body at 5:00 PM. It was 3:15, and we were supposed to be at the famous "Bronze Doors" designed by Michelangelo at 4:30 wearing cassock and surplice.

None of us had said Mass yet that day and knew that the evening was going to be unpredictable, so we decided to say Mass first and then trust Divine Providence to get us down to the Vatican through the colossal traffic jam at the Tiber. We headed to our little private Mass chapel at the Casa Santa Maria and celebrated the Mass for the Solemnity of the Annunciation, transferred from March 25 this year because it fell on Good Friday. I asked Our Lady to help me to be, with the pope, *totus tuus*, "totally yours," and entrusted the rest of the day to her maternal care.

After Mass and a quick thanksgiving, we dashed out the door and grabbed the first taxi we saw and shouted, "*Vaticano!*" to the driver. We headed into a sea of traffic, and for nearly ten minutes we went nowhere. It was now nearly 4:15 and we knew we were pushing our luck for getting to the Bronze Doors by 4:30. At one point we nearly got out of the cab and started walking due to the bumper-to-bumper traffic. As we sat at a red light, I looked out the left-hand window and saw Cardinal Ruini, Vicar General of the diocese of Rome, in the back seat of the car next to me. He looked up and the three of us waved to him. He nodded in return, then the light turned green and his driver sped off behind a police escort. Behind Cardinal Ruini's car were three more cars carrying a total of seven cardinals! We decided we couldn't be that late if the cardinals were still rushing back to the Vatican for the procession, but we had no police escort and the clock was ticking.

When we got about a mile from the Vatican, we encountered a new obstacle, a roadblock which was set up to divert all traffic to the north and around the bridge that goes directly to the Vatican. The three of us rolled the window down, shouted, "*Per la processione!*" ("For the procession!") to the two officers, and they proceeded to wave us past the roadblock and down the empty Corso Vittorio Emmanuele straight toward the Vatican! We were going to make it!

The bridge across the Tiber was completely closed, so we hopped out, paid the driver and dashed across the bridge. A cameraman (there are cameramen *everywhere* around St. Peter's) started snapping photos of the three of us in cassocks running across the bridge. I hope they turned out for him! That was definitely the most memorable taxi ride I have ever had.

In a few minutes we made it to the Bronze Doors, the Swiss Guards saluted us and then they directed us up to a "waiting room" on the second floor, a huge sixteenth-century Renaissance hall with walls painted to depict different stories from the Old Testament. There were at least two thousand priests in the hall. I will now try to explain a truly extraordinary moment that for me has captured the beauty, history, depth, solemnity and spiritual power of the Catholic Church more than any I have ever experienced in my life.

After forty-five minutes of waiting, the massive bell in St. Peter's Square began to toll. We could hear it clearly through an open window. Then the Vatican choir began chanting, in Latin, "I am the resurrection and the life: he who believes in me, even if he dies, will live, and all who live and believe in me, will never die." The Cardinal Camerlengo (chamberlain), who oversees the Vatican during these days when there is no pope, began a prayer of blessing and sprinkled the pope's body with holy water (we could see none of this but only heard the audio portion that was being broadcast in the square). Every seven seconds or so, the huge bell tolled on. Then another prayer was read, which I will translate here in full. These are ancient prayers filled with beauty, sorrow and emotion at the death of the Roman pontiff:

> Beloved brothers and sisters, with great commotion of soul we now prayerfully translate the body of the Roman Pontiff John Paul II into the Vatican basilica, where he so often acted in his office as bishop of the Church which is at Rome and as shepherd of the universal Church.
>
> As we descend from this house, we give thanks to the Lord for the numerous gifts he has bestowed upon the Christian people through his servant Pope John Paul, and we implore him that he would graciously and mercifully grant to the supreme pontiff a perpetual seat in the kingdom of heaven and the consolation of supernatural hope to the pontifical family, God's holy people who live in Rome and to the Christian faithful throughout the world.

Then, after a moment of silence:

> Look kindly, O Lord, upon the life and work of your servant, our Pope John Paul II; accept him into your house of perpetual light and peace, and grant to your faithful

people that they would eagerly follow his footsteps in giving testimony to the gospel of Christ. You who live and reign forever and ever. Amen.[2]

These are profound and beautiful words, asking God to give the pope, who sat for a time on the Chair of Peter on earth, a perpetual chair or seat in heaven; asking that as he leaves his house (the papal apartments where he lived and worked) he will be accepted into the house of heaven; and especially praying for the Church of Rome and the papal household, now grieving at the loss of their head; and for the universal Church.

Then the deacon chanted, "Let us go in peace," and we responded, "In the name of Christ. Amen." And thus the procession began.

There was never a moment when we could actually see the entire procession. In fact, I have no idea what was at the front of the procession. But we slowly began to move as the choir began chanting Psalm 23 and then Psalm 51 in Latin, with the antiphon repeated over and over, "The bones that were crushed shall be exalted by the Lord." The melody was in a haunting minor key that captured the grief and also solemn nature of this moment in a way that only Gregorian chant could.

We went through two long painted hallways, then down an arched flight of stairs, through another corridor, down another flight of stairs, which turned to the left, and as I rounded the corner I gasped. We were at the top of the Scala Regia, designed by Michelangelo, and all the way down the cavernous arched hallway to the Bronze Doors, a distance of almost two hundred yards, there were priests as far as I could see. We processed four-by-four—I guess that I was looking at between two and three thousand priests just in that moment.

Down the stairs we went, step by ponderous step, as the bell tolled with finality and the chant continued, "The bones that were crushed shall be exalted by the Lord." After nearly ten minutes, when I reached the Doors, I turned back and saw priests extending far behind me. Way at the top of the stairs I could see the purple of the monsignors and bishops who were processing behind us, and just as we came out into the Square I thought I could see the first red birettas (square pointed hats) of the cardinals, who were nearly ninety in number.

The view looking back up Michelangelo's Scala, the hundreds of priests and bishops, coupled with the chant and the tolling bell, was a vision of something out of the ages. I had chills as we exited the doors, descended the final stairs and turned sharply to the right.

Out we came into the square, filled with four hundred thousand people straining for a glimpse. The procession crossed the square under the obelisk of Nero before turning right again to ascend the stairs to the main doors of St. Peter's Basilica. In one sense it looked like every other time people had gathered in those same spots to see the popemobile coming by and to wave and cheer and yell. But this time there was complete silence from the people as the chanting and tolling inexorably continued.

As the front of the procession came to the entrance to the basilica, the choir began the Litany of the Saints. Almost at the same time, the large JumboTron screens on either side of the Square showed the pope's body coming into view way back at the top of the Scala Regia behind the Bronze Doors. The body was carried by eight pallbearers of the papal household with white gloves, surrounded by six Swiss Guards in full ceremonial dress carrying halberds, followed by the papal household: several priests and bishops as well as the Polish nuns who cared for Pope John Paul. Ahead of the body were the Cardinal Camerlengo and the deacon in a gold and red cope of exquisitely detailed embroidery.

We slowly began ascending the steps of the basilica toward the towering central doors. The Litany of the Saints is so powerful, invoking name after name of the great ones who have gone before us in death and now share life with Christ in glory. Instead of the normal response, "*Ora pro nobis*" (Pray for us), we sang, "*Ora pro eo*" (Pray for him). The Blessed Virgin Mary, the angels and archangels, Saint Joseph, Saint John the Baptist and all twelve apostles were invoked one by one, and then all of the ancient pope saints: "Sancte Clemens, *ora pro eo*. Sancte Fabiane, *ora pro eo*. Sancte Leo Magne, *ora pro eo*. Sancte Gregori Magne, *ora pro eo*...." A dozen different popes, twenty-six martyrs and thirty-four other saints were invoked.

As we entered the basilica, it struck me that we were passing directly underneath the balcony where John Paul II had first been introduced to the world on October 16, 1978. Now he was entering the basilica for the last time to rest in peace awaiting the resurrection of the dead.

The pageantry and drama of this moment defy my ability to describe, but I hope this description can give just a glimpse of what it involved.

On entering the basilica, all the priests peeled off to each side and lined the center of the nave, forming two rows on either side, three priests deep. There was a pause as the body was turned around on the front steps of the basilica for the people to view. Then each cardinal came in one by one. I felt such a call to pray for these men who are now entrusted with caring for the Church and electing the next pope. At the back of the line of cardinals came Cardinal Sodano, Secretary of State under John Paul II, and Cardinal Ratzinger, Dean of the Sacred College, who will be the celebrant of Friday's funeral.

And then, as the bell kept tolling and the litany continued with prayers for God to have mercy on him, the body of the pope entered the basilica. His priests, who were ever so dear to his heart, were welcoming him. I begged his intercession for many graces as he went by.

I must say that the appearance of his body was not pleasant (he was not embalmed), and the memory of it has served as a meditation for me on the horror of sin. We know from Scripture that death is the result of sin. We are all of us, even John Paul the Great, under the dominion of death because of sin, and only Christ in the power of his resurrection can free us from the evil one. These days of mourning, occurring during the very beginning of the Easter season, are making me long for the resurrection with a greater yearning than ever before.

My response to seeing the pope pass by in death was, "This is not how it is supposed to be! We are made for life!" Certainly no one knew that better than John Paul II. And if he stood in need of our prayers while he exercised his ministry here on earth, how much more are we called to pray for him in a new way now that he has gone beyond the veil, even as he is undoubtedly praying for us in a new way now that he is with the Lord.

The procession reached the front of the basilica. The body was laid on the bier that had been prepared, surrounded by the Swiss Guards standing at attention and in prayer. A brief Gospel was read, Our Lord's words from Saint John: "Father, I desire that they also, whom you have given me, may be with me where I am, to behold my glory, which you have given me in your love for me before the foundation of the world" (John 17:24). Then a few petitions were offered, the Pater Noster was chanted and the Camerlengo concluded, "Eternal rest grant unto him, O Lord. And let perpetual light shine upon him. May he rest in peace. Amen." And with that a deep silence fell over the basilica. Thus began the vigil of prayer before the pope's body, still going on as I write these words two days later.

After the cardinals and bishops, all the priests were allowed to come up in fours and pass before the body. I genuflected, made the Sign of the Cross and held onto a special rosary that a priest at the Sanctuary of Divine Mercy in Krakow, Poland, gave me in 2003. We were not allowed to stop anywhere near the body, due to the tens of thousands of people waiting outside to come in (which became hundreds of thousands and now millions). But I found a quiet corner near the back of the basilica, knelt down and bid John Paul farewell. There was such a spirit of prayer and reverence in the basilica, which has continued today even as eighteen thousand people per hour are passing by. This is, I think, a testament to the unmatched ability of John Paul II, even in death, to lead people to encounter Jesus Christ.

I was asked by a reporter yesterday to sum up what this event means for me personally. My response was, "My youth is over." I grew up with John Paul II as pope, discerned my vocation by reading his writings, heard Christ calling me through him at Denver in 1993, followed him to Paris in 1997, to Rome for the Great Jubilee 2000, to Toronto in 2002 and I have lived with him for the past three years in Rome, often seeing him once a week at the Sunday Angelus address in St. Peter's

Square. For the rest of my life I will remember that, when I was young, John Paul the Great was the pope. It would be impossible for me to exaggerate the influence he has had on my life and particularly on my priestly vocation. He was and is my hero. This is true for an entire generation of young clergy who accompanied his body into the basilica on Monday night. My prayer at Mass beside his body today was that I would be half or even a quarter of the priest he was. I pray that God grant that request not only for me but also for all of our priests. Let us pray for his eternal rest, and for the whole Church, that the gift and Spirit of Christ, which John Paul bestowed on us through the Petrine ministry, will continue to bear fruit in the Church for years and years to come.

P.S. As yet I have no idea where I will end up during the papal funeral. Any prayers to Our Lady of Czestochowa that she will put me where she wants me to be would be greatly appreciated!

Among the countless young men who were influenced by Pope John Paul, many heard within them the loving call of Christ inviting them to enter the priesthood. The "JPII generation" of priests and seminarians continually looks to the late Holy Father as their model and hero as they pour out their lives in service to the Church. Their testimonies here bear witness to the fact that the Spirit which anointed the priesthood of John Paul II has been poured out a hundredfold on his spiritual sons.

The Moment That Changed My Entire Life

Father Jeffrey Njus, Michigan

Standing at the altar at my first Mass, I looked back on my life with wonder to see how God had brought me to that moment. I don't know how it would have been possible if not for a moment of encounter with Pope John Paul the Great.

I grew up in a faith-filled Christian home, but it wasn't a Catholic one. During college I went on a study tour that brought me to several countries around the Mediterranean. At one point our group of students stopped in Rome for a four-day layover. Thanks be to God, one of those days happened to be a Wednesday.

Every Wednesday morning the Holy Father has a general audience where he greets the pilgrims and tourists gathered in Rome. Someone told us to get there early and to try to get a spot on the aisle, so that's what we did. We arrived about an hour early, and I hurried down the row of chairs to get to the aisle. After waiting for about an hour, we all turned to the back of the hall as the doors were opened, and we saw Pope John Paul the Great walk into the room. As he made his way down the aisle, the pope would stop briefly at different points to greet someone or to bless a religious article. When he got to where I was standing, he didn't say anything to me, but he did stop to speak to the woman next to me. Meanwhile, I stood there holding his hand for a few moments.

That encounter with Pope John Paul was surprisingly moving for me. I knew that it would be significant to see the pope. But I thought that it would be more like seeing a president or another political dignitary. I didn't expect to be so spiritually moved by the experience. In fact, as Pope John Paul continued to make his way down the aisle, I could barely stand. I sat down and tried to collect myself. I knew in that moment that something powerful had happened. I would not have said that day that I would become a Catholic, and I certainly would not have said that I would become a priest. But I would have said even then that this had something to do with what God wanted me to do. That was the sense that I had that day—that moment had something to do with God's will for me.

That encounter planted the seeds of conversion and vocation in my heart. After talking with a lot of people and wrestling with a number of questions, a year after my encounter with Pope John Paul, I became Catholic. Ten years later, I became a priest.

Along the way, I wondered what exactly had happened in that moment of encounter with Pope John Paul. Another encounter with Pope John Paul years later helped me to understand. Shortly before I was ordained a priest, I was in Rome again. This time I was traveling with a group of seminarians. Our dream was to attend Mass with the Holy Father in his private chapel, and our dream came true. We walked into the chapel early that morning to find Pope John Paul kneeling in prayer before the tabernacle and an icon of Our Lady of Czestochowa. I ended up in the seat right behind him and I felt drawn into his prayer.

I realized that day that when I had encountered Pope John Paul the first time, I had not only encountered him. I had encountered Jesus Christ. Every morning the Holy Father opened his heart to Christ and offered himself to do God's will. In a mysterious way, when I touched the pope's hand, I was inspired to open my own heart to Christ and to offer myself to do God's will. What I encountered that day in Rome when I encountered Pope John Paul was holiness. The One whom I encountered that day was Christ.

Now as a priest, I kneel each morning in prayer before the tabernacle and before an icon of Mother Mary. I continue to be inspired by Pope John Paul the Great. I open my heart to Christ and pray that each day others will encounter Christ in me as I encountered Christ in Pope John Paul.

Suffering Servant

Father Jeremy Leatherby, California

When my vocation director contacted me and told me that my bishop had decided to send me to Rome to study for the priesthood, I was elated. Many thoughts arose in my mind, and an array of emotions stirred in my heart. I realized that one of my greatest dreams could possibly be fulfilled—my hope of meeting Pope John Paul II in person.

During my high school and college years, as I underwent an interior conversion of soul, I become strongly attracted to everything for which John Paul II stood. His relentless search for truth, his commitment to holiness of life and his tremendous love for Jesus Christ had captivated my heart. When I heard his incessant calls to his flock to "be saints" and to "be not afraid," I longed to respond. He inspired me and challenged me from afar to follow Jesus radically, and his witness and example gave me courage to do so. For this reason he became my greatest hero.

My first year and a half in Rome went by without my desire being fulfilled. As the Holy Father's health continued to decline, I faced the fact that perhaps I would have to wait until heaven in order to meet him. Yet unexpectedly in January, 2003, a call arrived at my seminary notifying us that we would be admitted to a private audience with John Paul II the following day. I couldn't wait for the moment.

The next morning as I entered the library of the papal palace and saw the Holy Father sitting across the room, tears filled my eyes. There sat my childhood hero. Yet he was not the vigorous and strong John Paul II that I had seen as a child. He was an elderly, hunched-over, tired man. I wanted to cry. It was as if this image of him might shatter the joy and excitement of the occasion. However, no tears rolled down my cheeks. Something prevented me from crying. A picture above the pope caught my attention, a painting of the crucifixion. As I gazed upon the depiction of Jesus dying on the cross, and then once again looked at John Paul II, my sadness turned to joy. I saw in him the suffering Christ, saving the world from its sin. It was as if John the Baptist was calling out again: "'Behold, the Lamb of God, who takes away the sin of the world'" (John 1:29). The Vicar of Christ, the representative of Christ on earth, seemed to me to be witnessing to Christ most fully at that moment. He was sharing in his passion.

I hardly recall the rest of the visit. Yes, I knelt before John Paul II, I received a rosary from him, and he lovingly patted me on the top of my head, as if he were my grandfather. I was in his presence. I touched him and smiled at him, but this was no longer the important aspect of the visit. Something deeper was engraved upon my heart after being in his presence. I had seen Christ personified in a man, the realization of the Christian vocation. I had also seen what God was calling me to become as a priest: another Christ, *alter Christus*.

That brief period of time with John Paul II will remain in my heart and mind as long as I live. It was not what I expected, but more than I could have dreamed of. I was ordained a priest in June 2006. If someone were to ask me for an image of the priesthood, I would describe John Paul II as he sat that day with his suffering and crippled body underneath Christ crucified. He is the priest whom I want to emulate. He is my hero.

Viva il Papa

Father David Toups, Florida

Having received my First Holy Communion the year Pope John Paul II was elected supreme pontiff, I consider myself to be right in the heart of the John Paul II generation.

From the earliest moments of my own living out of the Catholic faith, the life and witness of John Paul II helped inspire and encourage my own Christian vocation and ultimately my journey to consecrated service in the Church as a priest. I was privileged to have spent a total of seven years in Rome both as a seminarian and then as a post-graduate student priest. This proximity to the pope allowed numerous opportunities to see him with the thousands of pilgrims who flocked each year to the

Eternal City to pray with the 264 successor of Saint Peter. There were also moments of personal encounter—my classmates and I praying the rosary with him in a small chapel inside the Vatican, morning Mass in his private chapel in the Apostolic Palace, serving Mass for him in St. Peter's Basilica—but allow me to focus on the first time and the last time I was in his presence.

The year was 1993, and the Holy Father was coming to America for World Youth Day in Denver, a trip that many people thought would be a flop, "because the youth in America weren't interested in an old man from Rome." Were they ever wrong—one million strong, young people from all over the world came and cheered and prayed with Pope John Paul II. I was a seminarian at the time and accompanied a youth group from my diocese. The city of Denver was brought to a standstill, but there was no drunken carousing, no fights, in fact, no crime whatsoever. Instead there was joy, prayer and Christian fellowship. The media did not know what to make of it.

The pope flew into Mile High Stadium in a helicopter and circled around getting a view of his "fans"—the children of God, the souls entrusted to his care. When he landed, the volume of cheering had to rival that of any professional sporting event. "John Paul II, we love you!" was a favorite chant of the WYD participants; he engaged the crowds by responding, "And John Paul II, he loves *you!*" He spoke words of encouragement, words of hope to a generation thirsting for the truth.

He reminded us that Jesus invites all to partake fully in life—the Christian message is about being fully human, fully alive. The theme of that World Youth Day was John 10:10: "I came that they may have life, and have it abundantly." We, the JPII generation, are looking for the Truth and are ready to be challenged by the gospel message. John Paul trusted us, not as the future of the Church, but as the Church of the present:

> Young pilgrims, Christ needs you to enlighten the world and to show it the "path to life." The challenge is to make the Church's "yes" to life concrete and effective. The struggle will be long, and it needs each one of you. Place your intelligence, your talents, your enthusiasm, your compassion and your fortitude at the service of life! Have no fear.[3]

In 2004 a much slower and less energetic John Paul was still leading the Church with love and care. The day after defending my doctorate in sacred theology at the Holy Father's *alma mater,* the Angelicum, my parents and I were invited to a private audience with His Holiness. I knew that this would be the last time I would see my spiritual father in this life, and it was particularly special to share that moment with my parents.

Our hearts pounding, the three of us stood there waiting to approach the pope in his chair. As I approached him, his soft and warm blue eyes greeted me and I kissed the ring of the fisherman as a sign of my filial love and respect. I then handed him a copy of my newly minted thesis. I thanked him for his priestly example and for all that he had done and written on the renewal of the priesthood, which was my thesis topic. He smiled, nodded saying "gooood" in his deep Polish accent, handed me a rosary and then offered me a blessing. I then stepped aside and presented my mother to him and his face lit up as he said, "Ah, la Mamma!" nodding and blessing her. Finally, my earthly father and my spiritual father were face to face; tears welled up in my own dad's face seeing the aging and ailing pope. He felt his love being expressed to our whole family as he again blessed the three of us standing together in front of him. We walked away in silence, elated but numb from the experience. When one is in the presence of great holiness, it marks the soul for life.

Whoever has been given the privilege of standing before John Paul the Great knows that they were in the presence of a holy mystic, a beloved son of God who represented the Lord faithfully during his own earthly pilgrimage. The crowds would always cry to him, "*Viva il Papa!*"—"Long live the pope!" Now he is truly living forever in his eternal reward. John Paul II, we truly do love you. Holy Father, intercede for us.

Everything Is Grace

Father Bjorn Lundberg, Virginia

"Dear young people: John Paul II, he loves you!" With a roar of approval, tens of thousands of young people rejoiced with Pope John Paul II in Denver, Colorado. Gathered for the 1993 World Youth Day, we had come from the four corners of the world to see Saint Peter's successor and rejoice in our Catholic faith. As Pope John Paul was leaving the Saturday evening vigil at Cherry Creek State Park, he said farewell to all of us who were camping out. As we did so often that week, we hoarsely cried, "John Paul II, we love you!" over and over again.

Leaving the stage, he paused to tell us he loved us. We screamed, laughed and reveled in the moment of this encounter between the Holy Father and his enthusiastic children. There was a connection that was hard to explain. It captured our love and the growing faith we were discovering as young people of the third millennium. This was just the beginning of a special connection to Pope John Paul II that unfolded in my life during the next few years.

My love for the successor of Peter was strengthened after my freshman year of college when a group of students and friends traveled on pilgrimage to Rome to experience firsthand the faith and history we had read of in books. We especially enjoyed the public audience with Pope John Paul in St. Peter's Square. Pressed up against a security railing, our little group shouted and waved as the Holy Father passed by, blessing us. For the second time, I saw the Holy Father and felt so proud to be Catholic, and grateful for the chance to be in his presence.

Upon my graduation from Christendom College in Virginia in 1997, my family and I traveled to Italy on a pilgrimage organized by the school. What had begun at World Youth Day in Denver seemed to come full circle: four years of formation, studies, prayer and growing together as the John Paul II generation.

During the trip an unexpected opportunity arose not only to attend the pope's weekly audience but also to have two special tickets to sit near the pope and greet him at the conclusion of the audience. Our chaplain would be joined by someone in our group, to be determined by lottery. My father—the only non-Catholic in the group—won the drawing. He generously attempted to share the ticket with a student, but we all agreed: It was his chance. So my Lutheran father met the Holy Father on the steps of St. Peter's and received his blessing. As a family we were proud of him and excited to shake the hand of the man who held the hand of Pope John Paul II.

After the pilgrimage ended, I stayed in Rome as an intern for Vatican Radio. On July 4 the highlight of the summer came. Several weeks before, working with one of the staff reporters for Vatican Radio's English programming, we had drafted a letter requesting the possibility to attend the pope's private Mass in his chapel at the Apostolic Palace. Already by then the pope's poor health had led to speculations about the length of his pontificate. My boss warned me not to get my hopes up, as the Holy Father's activities were being scaled back. We sent off the letter, prayed and waited.

Word finally came that we could attend the pope's private Mass.

While the priests in our group vested to concelebrate Mass, the rest of us quietly prepared and waited in a large antechamber. A monsignor approached me and asked if I was from Vatican Radio, and then if I was from the United States. I said yes, and then he smiled, walked away and returned holding a lectionary. "Will you read for Mass?" he asked. Stunned, I said yes. "Good," he replied. "Big, strong voice."

The entire morning was surreal. We entered the pope's chapel. There he was, the Vicar of Christ. Shortly, the Mass began. When it was time, I walked slowly from my seat and approached the altar, passing by the pope. My mouth went entirely dry, and I had little appreciation for the torturous names of the Old Testament reading. However, I made it through. After Mass concluded, we were ushered out to wait for the pope. After his thanksgiving, the pope appeared, radiant. The quiet, recollected, prayerful pope had been energized by the Mass. He moved down the line, greeting the pilgrims, quipping with them, encouraging each person and group. At the end of the line, I waited. I gave the pope greetings from everyone at Christendom, and he responded. Then the monsignor mentioned Vatican Radio. Because it was the first Saturday of the month, the pope would recite the rosary live on the radio. The pope said, "This evening, we will pray the rosary, 8:30."

I replied, "Yes, Holy Father, I will be there. Tonight."

He patted my arm and confirmed, "Tonight." Then the pope of the rosary moved on.

The events of that summer morning occurred during a time when I was wrestling with the idea of a vocation to the priesthood. In the spring of 2000 I sent in my application to the diocese of Arlington, Virginia. Three years later, in January 2003, another beautiful event marked my vocation's connection to Pope John Paul II.

Over the Christmas holidays I traveled to Rome with a group of seminarians and transitional deacons for a ten-day visit. Our group was blessed to be visiting during the Year of the Rosary, and Our Lady blessed us in a very special way: we received word we were to attend the pope's audience in the Apostolic Palace. When the day arrived and we were gathered outside the famous Bronze Doors, we received word from the Swiss Guards that there had been a mistake. We were not scheduled to see the Holy Father. Our group was not on the list, and we could not be admitted.

But then, miraculously, we received permission to attend anyway. With great rejoicing we proceeded past the Swiss Guards and climbed the massive stairway. The *americani* were on their way.

As we entered the room for the audience, a Christmas tree greeted us first, and then we approached the pope. One by one we approached to make the *baciamano*, the kiss on the Holy Father's hand. Each seminarian knelt, kissed the fisherman's ring and received a blessing and a rosary. With a final blessing, we departed, some weeping, a few floating. As we made our way down the grand staircase and gathered in the square below, we decided on the appropriate manner of thanks: Praying with our new papal rosaries, we honored Our Lady and thanked God for the gift of this day and blessing on our vocations.

As Saint Thérèse expressed it: "Everything is grace." The vocation to the priesthood, the gift of the faith and love for the successor of Peter are all unmerited, and, too often, unappreciated treasures of grace. From the joy of celebrating WYD in the Colorado countryside, to the glory of Rome, to the quiet, patient discernment of a call to the priesthood, each step of my journey has had a special connection to Pope John Paul II. When one is aware of his complete unworthiness, perhaps he can revel even more in the glory of these moments. These extraordinary memories are opportunities to thank God for his gifts, and to share the joy of the faith he has blessed us with, through Our Lady's intercession.

I Can Do All Things Through Christ Who Strengthens Me

Patrick M. Behm, Iowa

I have had the unique privilege of being in the presence of Pope John Paul II numerous times. I attended World Youth Day 2002 in Toronto, and I also studied in Rome for a semester in 2004. During that semester, I was able to attend a number of Masses, Angelus blessings and a general audience with the Holy Father. Those experiences were all powerful, but the most powerful of all was Midnight Mass in St. Peter's Basilica on Christmas Eve, 2004.

After waiting in the rain for two hours just to get into the church, the line—if you can call it that—finally began to move. The section of the "line" that I was in was among the last to be let into the Basilica. I was afraid that we were not going to fit and we would be left out in the rain to watch the Mass on television. Fortunately, we were ushered in and some quick-thinking people in our group spotted seats relatively close to the main altar in one of the areas off the main part of the church. Once inside we had to wait another two hours for Mass to begin.

During the course of the semester, I had seen Pope John Paul visibly struggle with his health and stamina. Many times I saw him start to deliver a homily only to stop and turn it over to a cardinal who finished for him. I felt that he was a living martyr.

Midnight Mass, however, was different. It was as if the Holy Father knew that it would be his last one and he wanted to go out with a bang. I remember saying to a brother seminarian how privileged we were in God's Providence to be at this Mass, because it would be the last Midnight Mass of Pope John Paul II. I did not say that it *could* be his last Midnight Mass, but that it *would* be. Others around me shared this sense.

I do not remember much of the homily the pope preached that night. The one thing that sticks in my mind, though, was that he made it through the entire Eucharistic Prayer, audibly speaking the words of the Consecration. I have no doubt that our Lord was showering the pope with a multitude of graces, giving him the strength that he needed. By the end of the Mass, there was a not a dry eye in the basilica.

My experience of the final Midnight Mass of the papacy of John Paul II reminded me of so much he had taught us. When married couples from all over the globe brought the humble gifts of bread and wine to the Holy Father, I thought about his teachings on the sanctity of marriage. When God then turned those humble gifts of bread and wine into the Body and Blood of Christ himself through the hands of his servant Pope John Paul, I remembered the Holy Father's continual love and encouragement for his priests. The entire Mass brought home his constant call to conversion, his constant challenge of holiness in an age that often only challenges young people to follow the motto "If it feels good, do it."

Pope John Paul II has influenced my decision to study for the priesthood in so many ways; it would be impossible to describe them all. The pope's writings, teachings and unswerving witness to Christ and to the gospel have inspired me beyond words. John Paul II was willing to challenge the people of my generation. While other world leaders challenge young people to practice "safe sex," John Paul II instructed us on the dignity of each and every human person and the value of human sexuality, explaining the beauty of marriage. While other leaders promote "freedom of choice" via abortion, Pope John Paul consistently taught that each and every human person is created in the image and likeness of God and is thus entitled to life. While other leaders try to exclude God from our society, John Paul II preached that God is real and that he is actively working in our lives and has a plan for us. He told us we should "Be not afraid!"

In my humble estimation, Pope John Paul II was the greatest world leader of the twentieth century. Beyond that, I also believe John Paul II was the greatest witness and martyr for Christ of the twentieth century. Even in the twilight of his life, the Holy Father continued to reiterate in word and in action that we should not be afraid to follow Christ and to give our lives to him. His struggle to simply make it through Midnight Mass taught me that no matter what challenges or sufferings the Lord asks me to endure, "I can do all things in him who strengthens me" (Philippians 4:13).

CHAPTER FIVE

"Arrivederci, Giovanni Paolo"

Lord, who reveals the Father's love by your death and Resurrection, we believe in you and confidently repeat to you today: Jesus, I trust in you, have mercy upon us and upon the whole world.

—Pope John Paul II[1]

Friday, April 8, 2005—ROME

There is a steady rain falling and the streets are empty…. The very heavens are joining in the flood of tears poured out in this holy city on this holy day. I must tell you that I feel I have no words tonight, only tears. Today was by far the most difficult day yet. But I will try to give some thoughts and a reflection on my own experience of this day of the funeral Mass and burial of the 264th successor of Saint Peter, Pope John Paul the Great.

Today had a finality to it that is weighing on all of us. It is finished. John Paul has bid us farewell and we have commended him not only to the earth but also to the mercy of God and to the communion of saints, which he is now part of in a new way. All through this week he was still visibly with us—his body was on display for the veneration of the masses in St. Peter's Basilica, and even today during the Funeral Mass he was still physically in St. Peter's Square. The crowds applauded and cheered and prayed and wept in his physical presence, as they had so many countless times before. But then the final commendation came and the pope's pallbearers, the same men of the papal household who had served as his ushers throughout his life, carried his simple wooden coffin from its place in front of the altar toward the great bronze doors of the basilica which will be John Paul's final resting place. The papal choirboys chanted the Magnificat, Mary's hymn of praise from the first chapter of Saint Luke's Gospel, concluding with a final "*Gloria Patri et Filio et Spiritui Sancto*," and as they did so, the pallbearers turned the coffin around for a final moment of veneration by the faithful. The crowd erupted in applause, as it had several times throughout the Mass, and after a long moment, as the organ and choir rang out a fanfare of acclamation, the pallbearers turned for the last time, carried the coffin through the scarlet curtains across the threshold of the basilica and disappeared.

The young actor Karol Wojtyla could not possibly have imagined a more dramatic departure from the stage that was his life, with the entire world watching, not only the visible assembly of the universal Church on earth but also the invisible assembly of the angels and saints in heaven. If St. Peter's Basilica was constructed to be an image of the splendor of the kingdom of heaven, then the carrying of John Paul's coffin across the threshold of the basilica today and out of sight was the moment that most powerfully captured the spiritual reality that these days have witnessed: the world has lost a prophet, in many ways *the* prophet of our times, and we will never be the same ever again. Doubtlessly the Church goes on, and the Holy Spirit will raise up for her a new shepherd to rule in the See of Peter, but this particular man and his unique charism and mission will not be repeated. And for that we both mourn and thank God for allowing us to have been witnesses of the witness. "The LORD gave, and the LORD has taken away; blessed be the name of the LORD" (Job 1:21). These words have been my meditation today, as well as Christ's final words to his apostles in the Gospel of Luke, "You are witnesses of these things" (Luke 24:48). Truly each one of us who have lived through these extraordinary days are witnesses to an event of biblical proportions, an event that calls us to strive more seriously to follow Christ and to proclaim to all humankind the divine mercy of God that has poured out such a flood of grace upon the whole world during this momentous time.

Today's Mass was preceded by an all-night vigil that involved the entire city of Rome. Over two million people covered the city and slept wherever they could find a patch of ground to unroll a blanket or two, keeping watch for the morning and the Mass for which we were all waiting. At 9:00 PM last night a vigil for young people was held at the Basilica of St. John Lateran, cathedral of the diocese of Rome. I arrived about 9:45 and found the *entire floor* of the gargantuan basilica covered with young students, mostly Italians between the ages of sixteen and twenty-five. The overflow crowd (at least fifty thousand) spilled over into the piazza in front of the basilica, where speakers and JumboTron screens allowed people to participate in the prayer vigil. Several young people spoke, including one seminarian from the diocese of Rome who said that he realized that John Paul will never be "replaced," but he prayed that the cardinals will elect a new pope who will follow Christ the way John Paul has done. "This is what we young people ask of you, our bishops and priests," the young seminarian said, "follow Christ the way John Paul has done!" All the youth erupted in applause and then began chanting *"Giovanni Paolo,"* as they had done so often before.

But then a new chant slowly began to fill the basilica: *"Santo!* (clap-clap-clap) *Santo!"* An almost universal acclamation has been heard from the people of God this week in the Eternal City: that John Paul II is a saint! It was a cry that was repeated several times today in the square, along with huge banners amidst the throngs of people reading, *"Santo subito,"* or "Sainthood soon." At one point Cardinal Ratzinger had to wait several minutes while this cry of "*Santo!*" flooded the square before he could continue with the prayers of commendation.

After the vigil last night, the young people processed with candles from St. John Lateran to the Circus Maximus, where the Romans used to hold chariot races in the shadow of the Palatine Hill. This huge open space was transformed into a campground for the night for over one hundred thousand people. As we walked there was a profound silence along the route. Groups near us prayed the rosary and sang quietly in French, Italian and English. All along the streets the Roman people opened their windows and lit candles to accompany us in prayer. Especially as we passed the Colosseum, the sea of candle-light, song and prayer created an atmosphere of abiding peace and the sense that we were witnessing one of the defining spiritual moments of our time.

I got home after 1:30 AM and was up again at 5:00 so that a group of priests from my house could leave at 5:30 to make our way down to the Vatican. We walked well clear of all the main approaches to St. Peter's, and at all the numerous security barricades the Italian police were most accommodating to help us get down to the square. This has been the case all week and has really been quite touching. Many of the priests from our house were able to attend the funeral Mass sitting in the front section of the square. In God's Providence one of my closest brother priests, a member of my Iesus Caritas priestly fraternity group, was able to get access to an apartment on the top floor of the first building outside of the colonnade on the right side of the Via della Conciliazione. And so all morning we were able to have a bird's-eye view of the entire spectacle from the balcony.

The view was astounding. We could see all the way back to the Tiber with its bridges jammed with pilgrims, up and down the entire Via della Conciliazione, and we had an unobstructed view of all of St. Peter's Square. Two years ago in Czestochowa, Poland, I prayed at the icon of the Black Madonna, Queen of Poland, that when Pope John Paul died she would allow me to attend his funeral. I think she answered that prayer today in spades!

With the help of binoculars we were able to watch President and Mrs. Bush, former Presidents Bush and Clinton, Prince Charles, Tony Blair, Jacques Chirac and many other kings and dignitaries arrive. It was striking to all of us what a diverse group of leaders and political viewpoints were represented in the diplomatic seats today: No other person could have gathered together so many dignitaries in such a peaceful and prayerful way. Various other Church leaders, Orthodox bishops, Anglican and Protestant clergy and leaders of non-Christian religions were present as well.

Even in death John Paul brought the nations and religions of the world together in a way that testifies to his moral authority and spiritual leadership, unparalleled in our time. As pope he was truly the "Holy Father" not only of the Catholic Church but also of all Christians and even of the whole world. His heart was filled with love for every human person, no matter how important or how seemingly insignificant, and it was his love that today was returned by the whole world in bidding him farewell.

I want to conclude by pointing out just a few of the more striking moments of the funeral Mass. First, the Litany of the Saints of the Church of Rome, sung as on Monday during the procession of the body into the basilica, invoking the intercession of those who have gone before John Paul and await his company at the heavenly banquet. Special additions to this litany were Saint Maximilian Kolbe, the Polish Franciscan martyr of Auschwitz whom John Paul canonized, Saint Charles Borromeo, the pope's baptismal patron and, right at the end, Saint Maria Faustina Kowalska, the Servant of Divine Mercy whom John Paul canonized on Mercy Sunday during the Great Jubilee of the year 2000.

Next, the commendation done by the patriarchs of the Eastern Catholic Churches, chanted in Greek as two bishops in ornate golden vestments incensed the coffin simultaneously. This solemn rite demonstrated visibly that the pope's flock includes not just the Latin or Western Church but also the Churches of the East whose spiritual patrimony comes from the ancient patriarchal Churches of Constantinople, Antioch and Alexandria. He is truly the universal shepherd. This moment had profound significance for John Paul II, the pope of

Rome who dedicated so much of his life to the realization of Christ's prayer, "That they may all be one" (John 17:21). As the mysterious chant filled the entire square, the patriarchs prayed a litany of Divine Mercy, asking God for eternal rest for Pope John Paul, the forgiveness of all his sins and a place in the kingdom of heaven with all the saints. The litany concluded with the following haunting words chanted three times in Greek, "Eternal is your memory, our brother, you who are worthy of blessedness and unforgettable. Amen."

And finally, Cardinal Ratzinger's beautiful homily, in which he meditated on the call of Christ to Peter after the Resurrection in John's Gospel, when Christ says to Peter, "Follow me" (John 21:19). Cardinal Ratzinger showed how Karol Wojtyla heard Christ's call to follow him as a young student, followed him into the seminary and priesthood, then to the episcopacy and finally in October, 1978, to the papacy. John Paul II lived in a powerful way the words of Christ, "Whoever seeks to gain his life will lose it, but whoever loses his life will preserve it" (Luke 17:33). His life was completely surrendered to the will of God as revealed to him through the call of the Church. With Peter, he stretched out his hands and allowed himself to be taken where he did not wish to go (John 21:18).

Said Cardinal Ratzinger of the pope, "He interpreted for us the Paschal Mystery as a mystery of divine mercy."[2] The pope's entire life was dedicated to pro-

claiming the mystery of Jesus Christ, born of Mary, crucified and risen from the dead, as the source of mercy
and healing for a wounded world. And then a beautiful
conclusion by the cardinal:

> None of us can ever forget how in that last Easter
> Sunday of his life, the Holy Father, marked by suffering,
> came once more to the window of the Apostolic Palace
> and one last time gave his blessing *urbi et orbi*. We can
> be sure that our beloved Pope is standing today at the
> window of the Father's house, that he sees us and blesses
> us. Yes, bless us, Holy Father. We entrust your dear soul
> to the Mother of God, your Mother, who guided you
> each day and who will guide you now to the eternal
> glory of her Son, our Lord Jesus Christ. Amen.[3]

A moment of final parting not unlike the one we have all
experienced today appears at the conclusion of *Lord of
the Rings* trilogy by J.R.R. Tolkien. The quest has been
accomplished, the last boat is setting sail across the
Western Sea, and the fellowship must bid farewell.
Gandalf says, "Well, here at last, dear friends, on the
shores of the Sea comes the end of our fellowship in
Middle-earth. Go in peace! I will not say: do not weep;
for not all tears are an evil."[4]

Today at last came the end of our fellowship with
John Paul II on this earth. Now he awaits us on the
shores of the Undying Lands. We weep today, but only
because our love is so great. The fire of faith and hope

burns through our tears and purifies them, the same fire which was kindled on Easter night and drives away all darkness from the valley of death in which we live. Jesus Christ, *Redemptor Hominis*, the Redeemer of Man, is the Alpha and Omega who says to us, "Fear not, I am the first and the last, and the living one; I died, and behold I am alive for evermore, and I have the keys of Death and Hades" (Revelation 1:18).

Farewell, Holy Father! Godspeed! We will never forget you, and we will always, always pray for you, as you will for us, until we meet again.

Ever dear to the heart of John Paul II were those called to religious life, those chosen souls called even in this life to live that spousal union with the Lamb that will be the life of all the saints in heaven. Here a few of his spiritual daughters who have embraced consecrated life, as well as those discerning this beautiful call, share the way in which John Paul the Great opened their hearts to the love that has captivated them.

Glimpsing a Star

Nicole Morlok, Iowa

The way people talked about Pope John Paul II after they had seen him or met him was the way people talked about seeing movie stars or popular singers. People gushed about him. It made me wonder, "What is it about this man that makes people respond this way?"

I was a sophomore in college at the University of Nebraska in 2002 when I began to hear about the upcoming World Youth Day in Toronto. My closest friend—who was already a John Paul II fanatic—insisted that we should go and that I would love it.

Growing up, I didn't learn much about the pope, his role in my life or in the life of the Church, so when my friend excitedly told me about World Youth Day, I wasn't particularly enthusiastic. But a road trip to Canada with my friends and the opportunity to see young Catholics from all over the world seemed like it would be fun. I had grown a lot in my faith during my freshman and sophomore years of college. I was even starting to pray about God's will for my life and about my vocation, but I hadn't really found a personal connection with John Paul II. During the time before the trip I read about the pope, but I didn't think seeing him from miles away would change my life.

In Toronto I was amazed to see all the young adults who had come together to celebrate Jesus Christ and the Catholic faith. During the opening ceremony, my JPII-crazed friend and I were able to get within five feet of the barricades near the popemobile's path. I remember a rush of emotion as John Paul passed the crowd; everyone pushed to get closer. They wanted to be as close to him as possible.

I didn't make eye contact with him, but I found myself crying—tears were streaming down my face—and I had an immense desire in my heart to be holy and to have him be proud of me. I felt like a girl who loved her father so much that she desperately wanted his approval. Rarely have I wanted so strongly the good opinion of another person. I wanted to be able to tell him how I lived my life for God and have him tell me in return, "Yes, you have served our Lord well." It really was like a movie-star sighting, except that this star's holiness inspired those around him to desire to follow Christ completely.

At the closing Mass, I was exhausted, dirty and alternating between standing, sitting and kneeling in the muddy grass. During the pope's homily, I have to admit it was difficult to listen—I was praising God for the week in Toronto! After WYD I was going to be separated from some of my dearest friends as we each struck out on our individual paths. Suddenly, the pope's words cut into my thoughts. His words were as audible as if I was seated right next to him—it really was if he was speaking to me alone and directly into my ear. I will never forget the words that he said—"If you know in the depths of your heart that you are being called to the priesthood or con-secrated life, *do not be afraid* to follow Christ on the royal road of the Cross!"

At that point I *knew*. I wanted to ask the Holy Father, "How did you know I was called to religious life? Did you read my heart?" I wanted to do cartwheels, dance, shout and laugh all at the same time. I knew in the depths my heart that I was called to give my life to God completely in consecrated life. Through the Holy Father's words, the Lord confirmed what I had already been feeling. It was truly a moment of the outpouring of the Holy Spirit through the Vicar of Christ.

John Paul II fully awakened and brought forth my call. Reflecting on the previous two years, I clearly see how the Lord had been speaking to me and directing me to live a life consecrated to himself, but it wasn't until that moment in the mud at the closing World Youth Day Mass that I felt objectively called by the Lord and the Church.

I am so grateful that through my first encounter with John Paul II I heard the Lord calling me to love him in consecrated life. Like so many others, I discovered my vocation and the courage to follow it through John Paul II and his example. Now I not only want the Holy Father to be proud of me by being a holy Catholic, but also a holy religious sister. I ask John Paul's intercession to help me follow Christ on the royal road of the Cross so that one day we will all be together in heaven giving glory to God.

Loving Father

Sister Shawn Pauline of Carmel, O.C.D., California

Just as one drop of water cast into a still lake causes a ripple that affects the entire body of water, so too the life of Pope John Paul II affected the entire body of Christ, myself included. My name in religion is Sister Shawn Pauline of Carmel. By the tender grace of God I have been blessed to be named after one of the most saintly men of the 21st century. I would like to share a simple testimony of a daughter who was loved by her father and guided by his hand.

"Be not afraid." The one thing in life that I was most afraid of was having a religious vocation. I remember often at Mass during my teenage years I would cry when I heard the song "Be not afraid, I go before you always. Come follow me...." I knew God was calling me, and I *was* afraid. There was only one voice in the world that kept telling me *not* to be afraid, and it was John Paul II. His words, the very echo of Christ, planted the seeds of my vocation.

This voice continued to urge me onward, gently prodding me to look into religious life. When I went to the Franciscan University of Steubenville in the fall of 1998, I was bombarded with images and quotes of Pope John Paul II. I learned the phrases *"Coraggio,"* "John Paul II, we love you" and *"Totus tuus."* It was during this time that I began to understand the true greatness of this man, and the impact he had had on the entire world. Through the pope's example I grew in my relationship with Mary. I figured that if the pope said he is "totally Mary's" then I should be too. I committed my whole life to Mary through the Marian Consecration program on campus. The profound simplicity of his motto struck the core of my heart, and it was through the consecration that I really began to have a prayer life and follow Christ more closely. While at college I also met the Carmelite Sisters of the Most Sacred Heart of Los Angeles. We began a friendship, and slowly a deep respect and admiration for them was taking shape in my heart.

A few years went by. While spending a semester in Europe, I had the chance to see Pope John Paul II at a short weekly audience. From his balcony window he prayed the *Pater Noster* with us. I wept. An overwhelming awe at his words touched my soul. He spoke of the essence and desire of every person on earth: I am a child of the father and I am loved. In that first encounter those three words—father, child, love—adequately expressed the sense that overwhelmed my soul to the point of tears. I had seen God the Father in our pope; I knew I was his child, and I was changed forever.

His voice continued to urge me onward, gently prodding me to look into religious life. When I came back to the United States, I grew ever closer to God, and the friendship that had started with the sisters blossomed. It wasn't too long before I realized that God was calling me to California—but *I was afraid.*

Then one day I went to my mailbox to find a reply letter from the sister I had met at college, and in it she wrote one sentence that will forever be etched into my memory, "Do you realize that you have been privileged to live during the era of our saintly Holy Father, and now you are heeding his oft-repeated call to 'Be not afraid…'?" I remember that moment so clearly. I was stunned, shocked, for up until then I had not felt the impact of those words. It was because of him that I had the strength to overcome the fears that plagued my soul. The only thing that I could possibly do was to become a Carmelite sister.

After I finished my last semester of college in 2002 I had the great privilege to greet Pope John Paul II with my grandmother at another weekly audience in Rome. It was finally my chance to see my father face-to-face. I approached with a great peace, looked for a place to kneel and landed right in between his red shoes. Then as I knelt there I looked into the eyes of Pope John Paul II.

I was enraptured with his gaze—as if before the Eucharist—I just wanted to look at him. There are moments in life when words are very unnecessary—moments so intimate that words would tarnish them—and this was one of those. He looked at his child, smiled, reached out and grabbed my head and kissed me. Total peace flooded my soul, and then something strange went through my mind. I thought, "Why don't I get this excited to receive Jesus in the Eucharist? The pope is just a man, and the Eucharist is Christ himself."

I realize now that Pope John Paul II was a person whose humility immediately led you to Jesus. After meeting the pope, I had a strong sense that he wanted me to know that though meeting the Vicar of Christ is indeed an awesome experience, the encounter with Christ in the Eucharist is infinitely greater. I sensed that the Holy Father wanted me to know that *he* was only a man, a man who had responded to grace. The Holy Father led us all to Jesus and not to himself. That is why we loved him; that is why the whole world flocked to him. By his courageous love he chased away my fears and enabled me to encounter Christ. Blessed indeed is every soul who lived during the pontificate of Pope John Paul II, for we received his love, wisdom and guidance, and now we reap the benefits of his intercession from heaven. Forever we remain his beloved sons and daughters.

An Apple Pie for the Pope

Sister Gloria Therese, O.C.D., California

While taking a study break one Saturday afternoon in 1988, I joined my college roommate in front of the television, where she was watching coverage of one of the Marian Year pilgrimages of Pope John Paul II. She was overjoyed to watch him, and I admired her love and respect for the Saint Peter of our day. She was thousands of miles away from him, fifty years younger and even more distant in life experience, yet she loved him. I remember thinking, "He seems so distant from me. I would love to know him like she does."

A year after college I entered the Carmelite Sisters of the Most Sacred Heart of Los Angeles. After novitiate and temporary vows I formally asked permission to make my perpetual vows—my *forever*. During my entire journey of religious life, I was graced with Pope John Paul II as my good shepherd. His words and his life were an inspiration to me as I lived my life for Christ and his Church. With great joy I received the news that I would profess my final vows on July 18, 1999, the Year of God the Father in preparation for the Great Jubilee Year of 2000.

In April, 1999, I was asked to go to Rome to help with the Council of Major Superiors of Women Religious planning committee for World Youth Day 2000 and also to help with preparations for the dedication of the first American Sisters' House of Studies in Rome, the Domus Sanctae Mariae Guadalupe. More than forty sisters from the United States gathered at the Domus to help prepare for the dedication and for the all-American banquet that the sisters would serve to the cardinals, bishops and priests who had special roles in making the house of studies become a reality. My task was to cook, clean and make apple pies.

The pope's declining health prevented him from attending the dedication and dinner; however, I was told, with a bit of teasing, "If you make an apple pie for the Holy Father's weekly audience, we'll make sure it gets to him." Thus the night before the audience, I made him an apple pie and a card that said, "Holy Father, we love you. You are the apple of our eye." At seven o'clock the next morning, a group of ten mother generals and sisters of various congregations walked to St. Peter's Square— and I had the fresh apple pie and card in hand. We passed the Swiss Guards and the Holy Father's atten- dants as they eyed the pie and said in Italian, "That's for me, isn't it?" We were seated on the main platform near the pope. My prayer had come true. I was *close* to him, but little did I know that this prayer would be answered beyond all my expectations. After his address, it was time to depart, except for those who were invited to have a photo taken with the Holy Father.

When it was time to have our photograph taken, I was standing directly on the pope's right side, still holding the apple pie. Seeing an empty space at his right side, my mother general gently nudged me saying, "Go." I knelt at his feet with the pie in my hand. I saw his hand resting on the chair, so I bent down to kiss his ring. When I opened my eyes and lifted my head, he was looking directly into my eyes. We clasped hands and I said, "Holy Father, we love you." I then proceeded to put the pie in his lap. I tried to say, "All the sisters in America give this little gift to you," but after only one word, John Paul II made the sign of the cross on my forehead, and the pie was taken by one of the bishops.

When he blessed me I felt the power of God's Spirit move from the top of my head, through my entire body, down to my toes. I felt like a little girl at the feet of my grandfather, but at the same time I was profoundly aware that it was the blessing of Saint Peter himself. Then taking my face in his hands, he looked at me with radiant eyes and a little smile and said, "American sisters, American sisters." I couldn't move; I could only look into his loving eyes. The moment ended with a bishop on either side of me helping me to my feet, which I truly felt unable to do alone.

Yes, Pope John Paul II, you are the "apple of my eye," and every time we chant those words in the Divine Office, I *know* you are at my side.

CHAPTER SIX

Stories You Won't Hear on CNN

Your youth is not just your own property, your personal property or the property of a generation: it belongs to the whole of that space that every man traverses in his life's journey, and at the same time it is a special possession belonging to everyone. It is a possession of humanity itself. In you there is hope, for you belong to the future, just as the future belongs to you. For hope is always linked to the future; it is the expectation of "future good things." As a Christian virtue, it is linked to the expectation of those eternal good things which God has promised to man in Jesus Christ.

—Pope John Paul II[1]

Monday, April 11, 2005—ROME

It is now Monday morning, and the rain that began on Friday almost immediately after the funeral Mass continues to fall steadily. Remarkable, not only because of how these heavy, overcast skies rolled in at the very moment of John Paul's burial, but also because during the entire week when hundreds of thousands were keeping vigil during the pope's last hours, waiting in line to view his body and camping on the streets, not a drop of rain fell.

More than once I have experienced moments with John Paul II where dramatic weather timed itself perfectly to coincide with his speaking. A perfect rainbow appeared over Mile High Stadium in Denver on August 12, 1993, just as the pope led us at World Youth Day in singing the *Pater Noster*. A dramatic front swept over World Youth Day in Toronto on Sunday morning, July 28, 2002, transforming a torrential downpour into brilliant sunshine just as the Gospel was read and the pope began to preach. Even in death John Paul II has had a remarkable cooperation of the elements in forming the backdrop to his dramatic exit from the stage of life.

I want to share some of the numerous stories that are being passed around Rome this week, as we all take a deep breath and try to comprehend the monumental importance of the past ten days. They give just a glimpse of how much grace was being poured out on the Eternal City during the salvific moment of John Paul the Great's passing, to say nothing of the grace being poured out on the entire world as it watched from afar on its knees. These vignettes follow in no particular order and attempt to paint a picture in words, to the praise and glory of God, of the impact John Paul II has had on the Church and the whole world during his final days.

✝

Last week I personally met a group of students from Franciscan University of Steubenville (three busloads, to be precise!) who are spending the semester studying in Gaming, Austria. When news of the pope's death reached them, they spontaneously decided to come and get in line to view his body. The school administration cooperated with the students' initiative by canceling classes for two days. They chartered buses, left Austria at 5:00 PM on Monday evening, April 4, drove all night and arrived in Rome at 6:00 AM on Tuesday morning. They then immediately got in line and waited six hours to see the pope's body (a relatively short wait given conditions later in the week). They had several hours free in the afternoon—a few came to Mass at the chapel at my residence. Then at 7:00 PM they reboarded their buses and drove home to Austria, arriving at 8:00 AM on Wednesday morning…at which point they went to class.

Twenty-six hours in a bus, two consecutive nights without a bed or showers, six hours in line—all to walk past the body of the pope for a few brief seconds. I cannot tell you how inspired I was by the devotion and faith and love for the pope (to say nothing of the love for Christ) of these twenty- and twenty-one-year-olds. The future of the Church is bright based on this glimpse I had of the John Paul II generation in action.

✝

A priest who lives with me went down early one morning (about 4:00 AM) and got in line to view the pope's body. During the following hours as they waited together, he befriended a group of ten Spanish men, all university students who had spontaneously decided to hop on a plane from Madrid. As they talked to the priest, it became clear that none of them went to church regularly or practiced their faith, although as Spaniards all were baptized Catholics.

When they finally went past the pope's body, these young men all began crying, and then went to the side of St. Peter's Basilica where they could pray for a few moments. At this point, one of the young men asked the priest if he could go to confession. After he went, another asked the same question, and then one by one *all ten men* went to confession for the first time in many years. The priest spent about two hours listening, advising and absolving these students.

In God's Providence there can be no coincidences. I am confident that this story has been repeated hundreds if not thousands of times in the last week on the streets of Rome. Priests were hearing confessions all over this town, in the most unlikely places (again, reminiscent of conditions at the World Youth Days).

A Polish nun who works as sacristan at our house recounted the story of a Polish man who, after viewing the pope's body, went to confession for the first time in *forty-five years*!

An American woman who lives in Rome came down to the square on the night before the pope died, more out of curiosity than anything, and found herself standing next to a group of American high school students who prayed the rosary and knelt in prayer for nearly three straight hours from 9:00 PM to midnight. She was moved to tears, told one of the chaperones from their school that she had never witnessed anything more beautiful, and said that her entire life had been changed by those few hours in St. Peter's Square.

John Paul is bearing fruit in death apparently even more abundantly than he did in life. This should come to us as no surprise. Christ tells us: "Truly, truly, I say to you, unless a grain of wheat falls into the earth and dies, it remains alone; but if it dies, it bears much fruit" (John 12:24). What is true of Christ is no less true of his saints.

Speaking of saints, one of the best ideas I have heard yet is that John Paul II should be beatified as quickly as possible, and then he and Mother Teresa of Calcutta should be canonized together. The crowd for that Mass might even exceed last week's!

Inside St. Peter's Basilica, the Vatican grottoes underneath the main floor of the church have been closed since the funeral and will not open until later this week. John Paul was buried in these grottoes in the former crypt of Blessed John XXIII, whose relics were brought up into the main basilica when John Paul II beatified him during the Great Jubilee. It seems that the grottoes are remaining closed for a few days in an attempt to empty Rome of pilgrims and reduce the massive numbers of people who continue to visit the basilica.

But the Polish pilgrims will not be deterred! Each day there have been people kneeling at prayer throughout the day over the air vents that lead down to the grottoes from the floor of the main basilica. These round holes are covered with brass manhole-like covers that have holes in them, so that one can partially see through into the grottoes. On Monday morning at 7:15 there were over fifty people kneeling at these holes and praying, causing a bit of chaos for the St. Peter's altar servers trying to direct priests to the various altars for morning Mass. The veneration of the tomb of John Paul the Great has begun!

✝

Last week Sister Nirmala, successor to Mother Teresa as Mother General of the Missionaries of Charity, flew to Rome from Calcutta for the funeral. She came to the basilica to venerate the pope's body and sat near the bier in the back row of the chairs reserved for bishops and cardinals. After spending some time in prayer, she was getting up to leave when she brushed the arm of Bishop Stanislaw Dziwisz, the pope's personal secretary, who was of course at the pope's side when he died and spent many hours in prayer as the body lay in the basilica last week. When Bishop Dziwisz looked up and saw Sister Nirmala, he jumped up, took her arm, led her right up next to the body of the pope and let her kneel there for an extended period of prayer.

Certainly, as Mother General of the Missionaries of Charity, Sister Nirmala had a special relationship with John Paul II. But her relationship is in fact even more special. Here's why: Some years ago, Mother Teresa approached the pope with the idea that every one of her sisters would spiritually adopt a priest to pray for, in the same way that Saint Thérèse of the Child Jesus, the French Carmelite who died in Lisieux in 1897, adopted two priests as "spiritual brothers" whom she prayed for throughout her life. The pope wholeheartedly endorsed the idea, but then turned to Mother Teresa and said, "But Mother, *I* am a priest.... Who will adopt me?" Mother Teresa turned to her secretary and said, "Sister Nirmala will adopt you." And so last week, kneeling next to John Paul's body in St. Peter's Basilica, Sister Nirmala bade farewell to her adopted brother who was also her Holy Father.

✝

Each day this week, for nine consecutive days or *Novem Diales*, a solemn funeral Mass is being celebrated at the high altar of St. Peter's Basilica, and these Masses are attracting massive numbers of Romans and other pilgrims. I attended the Mass at five o'clock on Sunday evening, April 10, celebrated by Cardinal Ruini, Vicar

General for the diocese of Rome; it drew over thirty thousand people to the basilica with another twenty thousand overflow crowd outside, a larger number than any Easter or Christmas Mass in recent memory. The mayor of Rome announced yesterday that Rome's central train station, Stazione Termini, is going to be renamed Stazione Giovanni Paolo II. The response of the Roman people to the death of John Paul II continues to be astounding.

As the conclave approaches, let us not forget our serious duty to pray for the cardinal electors. A priest friend of mine saw an American cardinal in St. Peter's Basilica yesterday and called out, "We're praying for you, Your Eminence!" The cardinal stopped, grabbed the priest's hand, looked him straight in the eyes and whispered, "Please!" I think that sums up the weight on these men's shoulders in the coming days.

Each cardinal will make the following oath each time he individually casts his written vote: "I call as my witness Christ the Lord who will be my judge, that my vote is given to the one whom before God I think should be elected." Each cardinal will take this oath as he stands before Michelangelo's dramatic painting, *The Last Judgment*, in the Sistine Chapel. Pope John Paul specifically decreed in 1996 that the papal election must take place in the Sistine Chapel, "where everything is conducive to an awareness of the presence of God, in whose sight each person will one day be judged."[2] Let us pray that each cardinal will act in a way worthy of eternal reward from the Lord in the coming days.

✝

I want to close with a mysterious quotation from John Paul II about the dramatic days that are about to unfold for the Church. In 2003 Pope John Paul published three poems in a book called *Roman Triptych: Meditations.* The second poem is called "Meditations on the Book of Genesis at the Threshold of the Sistine Chapel." After powerful meditations on Creation (depicted on the ceiling) and the Last Judgment (depicted on the front wall), John Paul wrote an epilogue about the dramatic moment of the conclave, which takes place in what is perhaps the most powerful artistic space in the world. He takes the word *conclave,* meaning literally "with the keys" (a reference to the fact that the cardinals are locked in the Sistine Chapel), and gives it a spiritual interpretation, referring to the power of the keys given to Peter with which he governs Christ's Church.

His words serve as a profound meditation to us about the spiritual power at work in next week's conclave:

> Those entrusted with the legacy of the keys
> gather here, letting themselves be enfolded
> by the Sistine's colors,
> …
> and so it will be once more, when the time comes,
> after my death.

John Paul II, We Love You!

...

You who see all, point to him!
He will point him out.[3]

Even in his final days, John Paul II was still touching the souls of young people. Indeed, it seems that some of the most powerful graces of all were reserved by the Lord for those whom he called to be present in Rome during the time of his passing. These young people did not anticipate receiving this extraordinary grace, but they all feel that their experience of those momentous days has marked them forever.

Follow Me

Joan Marie Clare Watson, Indiana

I was blessed to have the opportunity to study in Rome during the spring of 2005 with twenty-eight of my Christendom College classmates. Throughout the first two months of our semester, my friends and I seized every chance we could to see the Holy Father. Because of his hospital stays, John Paul's public appearances had been suspended, but he continued to come to his window on Sundays at noon for the Angelus and on Wednesdays around 11:00 AM, the time of his usual public audiences.

My friends and I joined the hundreds of thousands of pilgrims in St. Peter's Square on Easter Sunday when he came to his window for the traditional *Urbi et Orbi* blessing. While we had seen him many times before, that Sunday was different. It was Easter, a time of joy, but when our Holy Father attempted to speak, he was unable to. A mixture of emotions ran through me. How could one man suffer so much? "If any man would come after me, let him deny himself and take up his cross and follow me" (Mark 8:34). John Paul did not come to his window so that I would protest the injustice of his suffering, but so that I would become more resigned to God's will in my own life.

On Wednesday, March 30, we returned to St. Peter's Square hoping to see John Paul again. As we headed into the piazza, we all agreed that we would be very blessed if he would come to his window that day. I suppose in our hearts we all knew his health was declining even more, given his unprecedented absence from the Holy Week Masses and his inability to speak on Easter. When we entered the square, the large televisions had a message in Italian confirming that the Holy Father would come to his window at 11:00 AM.

Around 11:05 the Holy Father's window opened and the crowd erupted in cheers. His arms seemed to be moving fairly freely, and he was blessing the crowd and waving. It wasn't until I looked at the television and was able to see his face clearly that I realized how much he was suffering. His appearance was brief, and everyone left in tears. I cannot remember a time when his pain was more evident. He was dying, but he still came to his window to greet his flock.

After years of reminding us, "Be not afraid!" he clearly did not fear death or suffering. He was not afraid to show his suffering to a world that has condemned suffering and forgotten the blessings attached to pain. It did not matter that he could not speak. His courage and acceptance of God's will needed no verbal explanation. He taught and inspired me through those two appearances in ways no words could have.

Every time I saw the Holy Father that semester, I told him good-bye in my heart. Each time I never let myself hope to see him again. That Wednesday we saw him for the last time on this earth. But I didn't have to tell him good-bye. As hard as it was to accept at first, he is closer to us now than he ever was before. While he was alive, we all felt like he knew us individually. Now he really does.

Blessed

Melissa Josephson, Wisconsin

I am not what one would call a "lucky" girl. I have never won a raffle or even a simple contest. I never thought that I would be able to see an important person or witness a significant moment in history. As a child, I did not really know a lot about Pope John Paul II, but after watching him on television and reading articles about him in newspapers and magazines, I had wished I could be one of the lucky people who could at least see him in person. I always felt a love for John Paul II, basically because of how he loved the youth. I felt special because I was a young person, and he loved me even though he did not know me personally. I had accepted the fact that

TV would be the only place where I would ever see him, but then God had another plan.

When I was a high school freshman in 2005, I had the opportunity to travel to Rome with my school, Trinity Academy. I knew that the pope was very sick and that no one had any idea how long he had to live, and I had a strong feeling that I had to go and see him.

It was March 25, 2005, Good Friday, when my school group arrived in Rome. I was told that after Mass on Easter Sunday the Holy Father was to make an appearance from his window. And so it was that on Easter morning I found myself waiting in the huge and overcrowded St. Peter's Square. It was hot and the sun was shining, not a cloud in the sky. People of different nationalities were all waiting for the same reason, the same person. Finally, a little after noon, the large shutters opened, and he was rolled up to the window in his chair.

His room was very high up and I had difficulty seeing. Using my digital camera, I zoomed in and snapped a pretty good picture. He had just had surgery and had difficulty speaking. When he came out, he could not speak at all. You could see, even from far away, that this hurt him deeply. However, this did not keep the crowd from an endless cheer, clapping, whistling and singing in many languages. Even though he could not speak, he raised his hand and gave the whole crowd a blessing with much difficulty. I had a rush that is unexplainable, even to this day. I had finally seen the Holy

Father in person, and I felt so blessed to be there on that day. All I could do is smile and happily cry. However, I was worried. He was so weak and fragile. All I could do was pray that he would be strong again and for a long time after that. But again, God had other plans.

We were still in Rome on April 1 when we heard that the Holy Father was dying. We were all shocked. We quickly called cabs and joined the many people who were already in St. Peter's Square, crying and praying as one family. You could hear the rosary being prayed in many different languages. We looked up at the light in his room, praying with all we had inside us that the light would remain on. People were handing out candles, and we lit them, holding the candles and praying.

The experience was indescribable. I cried along with the others, not believing that this was actually happening. It was getting very late, and we had to go back to the convent where we were staying. The next morning when we woke up, Pope John Paul II was still alive. We were all relieved. We took the bus back to St. Peter's Square.

We sat there and prayed with many others who had camped out there during the night. I stared up at the large windows, still in amazement. Yes, he was sick on Easter when I saw him, but I did not think that he was in that much danger. We had places that we had to see that day, so we began to leave. I took out my camera and took a picture of his windows, because as we left St. Peter's Square, I sorrowfully knew in my heart that the next time we were there the Holy Father would already have breathed his last.

That evening we heard the news. Pope John Paul II had died. We all were crushed. We went as quickly as we could to St. Peter's Square, to cry with thousands of others. I saw the young and the old, priests and laity. At that time, it did not hit me that Pope John Paul II was dead—the man that cared for so many, the living saint. The idea was unimaginable. I watched him on TV as a child, grew up knowing that he was a strong holy man whom even a bullet could not stop from completing his duty on earth. Yet, now he was gone. The light inside his room was off.

On Monday, April 4, we arrived in St. Peter's Square to witness the Holy Father lying in state. John Paul's body was to be carried in procession through the square and into the basilica. It was eleven o'clock in the morning. Some people were handing out water to those who were waiting in line to pay their last respects. We were told to not drink too much, because if we left the line to use the bathroom, we would have to go to the very end, not back to our original spot. So we drank sparingly. The line moved slowly. We waited in the blistering heat all day. We were tired and hungry, but we still waited.

The procession started. Many priests, bishops, cardinals came out, followed by the Swiss Guard with the deceased pope carried behind. I was lucky to see what was going on. If we had been a little later, we would have been stuck in line with the thousands of other people behind us who were not close enough to see the procession. We waited a while longer, and finally around 11:00 PM we were able to enter the basilica. Because of the extremely large crowd outside, we were moved steadily through. We were not allowed to stop for even a second.

As I looked at the Holy Father's body, he looked peaceful, and even though I was sad I felt an inner peace. The next morning when we left Rome to return to the United States, people were still lined up to see John Paul's body. I could not fully appreciate how blessed I was to have been there at that time.

Pope John Paul II still lives in my heart. I fully believe that he was sent by God to rescue the twentieth century from darkness. He taught people to love in the most unloving time in history. He showed compassion and love to all, even those of different races and religions. He is the biggest role model in my life. He showed me love and kindness that I had never seen before or imagined. Words cannot begin to describe the way he affected my life.

He Taught Me How to Pray

Marina Schumaker, Wisconsin

Pope John Paul II had a great impact on my life, and although I did not have the privilege of meeting him face-to-face, I was at his last Easter Blessing. I know many people have seen him close up at World Youth

Days, but I only saw him on television, so the importance of the pope did not have that much meaning to me—until my pilgrimage to Rome with my classmates for Easter, 2005. The pope has a different meaning to me now. He's the father of the Church, a role model for the entire world—and a friend.

Although standing in St. Peter's Square on Easter Sunday waiting for Pope John Paul II to come to his window was exciting, I didn't feel anything too emotional. When he came to the window, however, my faith and my emotions changed. Although he was in his window and I could barely see him, I still felt that he saw me among all of the other people in St. Peter's during that time. Although he could not even speak or finish the blessing, just seeing him was breathtaking, and the world seemed to stop. Never had I had so many feelings all mixed into one huge emotion that I still cannot explain. They were feelings of joy, but at the same time nervousness. There was excitement and amazement. Finally there was the feeling of happiness that I was given the gift to see this wonderful man whom I had heard so much about.

At this moment my faith became real to me, and from then on all of the prayers I said meant something. The Hail Mary wasn't something I just said to get through the rosary; it was something I meditated on. This was a new feeling of prayer really being powerful. He was the leader of the Church, and he cared so much for all of us as his family. Knowing that he was praying for me made me feel more secure and safe. I never thought prayer could affect my feelings this way.

The night that Pope John Paul II was dying was heartbreaking. I spent it kneeling and praying underneath his window where I knew that the world's most beloved man was inside suffering. Just thinking about that man who had changed the world through his example and love for everyone made tears pour down my face. Before the blessing he was my pope, but after the blessing and that night he became my role model and a person that I cared for more than I ever imagined. I was scared, because I thought, "What if he doesn't make it through? What is going to happen to this world and all of the good, holiness and peace he brought to it?"

Seeing how many appeared that night, knowing that many of them probably weren't even Catholic, was so amazingly beautiful. I asked myself, "Could this happen anywhere else but in the presence of Pope John Paul II?" That night I felt sorrow that he was suffering so, but also happiness that this man who suffered so much over the years and carried so many crosses throughout his life was finally going to be at peace and have his chance to go and be with the person he loved most, Jesus Christ.

I felt terrible that Pope John Paul II had such heavy crosses to bear and never complained about his sufferings, but we, who whine every day because we have homework to do or chores that have to be done, don't think twice about complaining about the crosses that we receive. He knew that he was given these crosses by God, and for that reason he took up his responsibility for them. He showed us how we need to accept the crosses God gives us because they will teach us. The crosses in our daily lives can teach us virtues such as patience and self-discipline and can help us be more charitable and prayerful in our daily lives. His example showed me how to thank the Lord for my crosses instead of complaining about them.

The next day was a day of reflection and silence. I did not feel like talking. I was just thinking and absorbing the news that Pope John Paul II had died. All day I was in line waiting to be able to view his body. It was hard to think that I was chosen, along with my classmates, to be there on that very significant day in history. Only tens of thousands of people were chosen out of the entire world to be able to view his body in person, and I was one of them. It was a sign from God. He wanted me to be there. It was not a coincidence, but God knew I needed something to strengthen my faith and he gave it to me.

After waiting in line for ten and a half hours to view his body, I got inside St. Peter's Basilica. Inside the church I did not know what to do, think or say. My mind froze into a sad state of happiness, for this man brought so much hope to this world. He gave the poor hope and sinners hope. He believed in the youth, that it was our duty to carry God's word out into the secular world, and he spread God's teachings everywhere he went. The center of his life was Christ. He gave everything to Christ and trusted that God would take care of whatever he needed.

As I walked past his body I could not help but stop and think about how my first trip to Rome was the most important in my entire life. I knew I would never have the same feelings ever again. Seeing him lie there, the world seemed empty and cold. As I looked at his body, I couldn't help but say a prayer, and that surprised me. I never thought that I would see Pope John Paul II, and even if I did, I never dreamed that I would say a prayer just because of seeing him. At this moment I knew I was changed. Prayer had become part of my life without my even realizing it.

CHAPTER SEVEN

"Habemus Papam!"

The Lamb who was slain is alive, bearing the marks of his Passion in the splendour of the Resurrection. He alone is master of all the events of history: he opens its "seals" (cf. Rev 5:1–10) and proclaims, in time and beyond, the power of life over death.

—Pope John Paul II[1]

Tuesday, April 19, 2005—ROME

Our Lord did indeed "point him out"—with astonishing rapidity and clarity. Just after six o'clock in the evening on April 19, 2005, barely twenty-four hours into the conclave, the bells of St. Peter's Basilica began pealing out news of tremendous, stupendous, unbounded joy—*Habemus Papam!* We have a pope!

Once again I found myself witnessing history in St. Peter's Square, although this time the emotions and sentiments experienced were of such a radically different nature as to make me marvel all the more at the mystery of the life of the Church. *Only* the Holy Spirit could transform such profound grief into such profound joy so radically and completely. The joy of the Resurrection, greatly subdued on Easter Sunday because of the visible and poignant suffering of John Paul II, finally descended in an unmistakably powerful way on Rome and on the entire Church on Tuesday of the third week of Easter.

Those of us who were privileged in God's mercy and providence to have experienced April, 2005, in Rome were participants in the paschal mystery of Christ—his suffering, death and resurrection—as it was lived by his body the Church through the passion and death of Christ's servant, Pope John Paul the Great.

On the day of the funeral, while walking home with a priest friend of mine, I had said to him, "I don't think I will ever be able to be happy again in St. Peter's Square." There were not words for our grief, nor did it seem there could ever be enough tears. I am sure that not since the road to Emmaus had there ever been two disciples as downcast and sad as we were that rainy afternoon.

The days following were quiet and reflective, as the solemn novena of Masses was offered for the repose of the Holy Father's soul each evening at the high altar in St. Peter's. There was an emptiness, a Holy-Saturday-like quality about those days. As the rain fell in Rome, something was missing, something that seemed irreplaceable. Although we knew there would be another pope elected shortly, there was a part of me that felt that whoever it would be couldn't possibly be the same. Would he

understand how much my generation had loved John
Paul II, how he was truly our spiritual father, how our
entire living of the gospel and our decision to follow
Christ with such intensity was all the result of John
Paul's challenging love for us?

I felt like a little child who wanted to say to all the big,
important cardinals, "I hope you know that the next
pope had better understand how much we loved John
Paul II and that we still do more than ever!" And as the
conclave opened and I attended the Mass of the Holy
Spirit celebrated by the cardinals, these sentiments only
increased in my heart. Yet at the bottom was a quiet trust
that Christ knew what he was doing, and that he had for
a long time been preparing the man who would be
chosen as successor to John Paul II.

And so with all of these thoughts and wonderings filling my heart, I found myself standing in St. Peter's
Square on the evening of Tuesday, April 19.

Never did I anticipate the sheer joy and absolute
human excitement of the moment of the election of the
new pope. The Catholic Church is a master of drama.
What other institution would expect thousands of
people, from archbishops to little old ladies to network
news anchors to pack into a crowded piazza and watch
for white smoke from a chimney? And *then* the drama of
knowing that there was a new pope, but for almost 45
minutes not knowing *who* it was—I challenge anyone

anywhere to come up with a more suspenseful electoral process!

That afternoon I found myself with a group of American college students in St. Peter's Square, shooting the breeze and never imagining that the election would happen so quickly. In fact, the students had an Italian test the next day, and their teacher had told them that *if* a pope got elected that night it would be canceled, but none of them were counting on that happening, and so they were all studying as we waited for what would certainly be black smoke to come out so we could go home for dinner.

And then just before six o'clock the chimney started smoking a nondescript color, and everyone started arguing about whether it was *bianco* or *nero* (they *gotta* get that taken care of for the next conclave!). I made my judgment more on the timing of the smoke than the color—there were supposed to be two ballots that evening and it seemed impossible that they could have finished so quickly, *unless* a pope had been elected on the first ballot! But we had also been told that the bells would start ringing to announce the election, and so I fixed my eyes on the huge bell on the left-hand side of the façade of St. Peter's, waiting for it to move.

Just before six o'clock, I said to some of the students with me, "It's going to ring six o'clock in a minute, and everyone will freak out and think it's for the new pope, but don't be fooled, it's only six o'clock!" And indeed on the stroke of six the *small* bells chimed out the hour as a roar of excitement went through the crowd...but I was determined to remain calm, cool and collected, unmoved by the false alarm.

And then, at 6:02, it started swinging. Even before it started ringing, back and forth it went, slowly at first, then faster and more intensely, and as the deep, loud voice of that mother of all bells began pealing out, I completely "lost it." All of my calm, cool, collectedness went up in (white) smoke as I began jumping and screaming for sheer joy and excitement as I *never* have before in my life, nor can I imagine ever being so excited in one specific moment about *anything* ever again.

Over and over and over again we all kept saying to one another, "We have a pope!" and screaming, I mean *screaming*, in excitement. And again I ask, what other institution could think something like this up? It was so hard to fathom that it was actually happening, and that I was actually standing in St. Peter's Square at this unbelievable moment, a moment that had last happened when I was four years old.

As the bells kept ringing and ringing and ringing, I helped make history by being one of the thousands who were the first people to ever make calls from cell phones while standing in St. Peter's Square at the moment of a papal election. It took me several tries to get through (there were probably only a few thousand other calls being made from the Square at the same time), but I was able to reach my family and a priest friend back in Nebraska. Both conversations consisted of screaming the words, "Guess where I'm standing?" as I shouted over the bells and the shouts of the crowd.

As the square kept filling up with people and the intensity and excitement impossibly kept growing, I suggested to the students with me that we pray the rosary for the new pope, whoever he was. They agreed, and I started the prayers, but I was so excited I could barely get the prayers out of my mouth—I was jumping up and down and screaming and looking around and saying, "Oh my goodness!" and "Can you believe it?" and a thousand other things. Halfway into the first decade, I asked a young lady if she would take over leading the prayers, and she very piously nodded and started leading, whereupon I very *un*piously went back to jumping and screaming. (Blessed Mother, please forgive me, but it's all Saint Peter's fault!)

When the moment finally came and Cardinal Jorge Medina Estevez, the Cardinal Proto-Deacon, came out onto the balcony, it was evident that he was enjoying every second of the suspenseful announcement. After milking every drop of excitement out of the crowd by saying "Dear brothers and sisters" in an array of languages, he announced to us the "great joy" of the news that we do indeed have a pope, "Dominum Iosephum Cardinalem Ratzinger...." I heard nothing else but bowed my head in prayer for dear Cardinal Ratzinger. "Oh Lord, please help him with your grace," I prayed, overwhelmed at the thought of the cross that had been laid on him and the burden of filling the shoes of John Paul.

And then, simply *beaming* with joy, Cardinal Ratzinger appeared on the balcony dressed up like the pope—no, wait a minute, he *was* the pope! I looked into one of the myriad television cameras that were all over the place and shouted, "Ratzinger's the pope!" Then we all began screaming and shouting and jumping even more crazily than before. We could not believe that it was true, and we were overjoyed beyond words at this gift from the Holy Spirit.

His new name was announced, Benedict XVI. My first thought was, "It's not very easy to make a cheer that rhymes with 'Benedict the sixteenth!'" And then as the crowd kept screaming with excitement, our new Holy Father inaugurated his pontificate with these beautiful words:

> Dear brothers and sisters, after the great Pope John Paul
> II, the cardinals have elected me, a simple and humble
> worker in the vineyard of the Lord. I am consoled by the
> fact that the Lord knows how to work and act even with
> insufficient instruments, and above all I entrust myself
> to your prayers. In the joy of the risen Lord, assured of
> his constant care, let us go forward. The Lord will help
> us, and Mary his Most Holy Mother will be at our side.
> Thank you.[2]

And then as the crowd began cheering for Papa "Benedetto," I marveled, absolutely marveled, at the goodness of God. Not only had the Holy Spirit given us a new Pope, but also he had removed completely whatever fears we of the "JPII generation" had that the new Holy Father might not understand how much John Paul the Great meant to us. Cardinal Ratzinger had been one of Pope John Paul's closest advisers and confidants for many, many years! His beautiful first words from the balcony made it clear that he understood that his role would be not only that of successor of Saint Peter but also that of successor of one of the greatest popes in the entire history of the Church.

With great, remarkable humility, Benedict made it clear that as Pope he would be the spiritual son of "the great Pope John Paul II," with whom he had worked so closely for so many years and to whom he now looked as a guide and prayerful intercessor from "the window of the Father's house." Indeed, in his address to the cardinals in the Sistine Chapel the following morning, he would make it clear to them that he attributed his election to a special grace obtained for him through the intercession of John Paul II.

With great trust and love Benedict would speak to his electors about how close he felt to John Paul II now that he was his successor as pope: "I seem to feel his strong hand clasping mine; I seem to see his smiling eyes and hear his words, at this moment addressed specifically to me, 'Do not be afraid!'"[3]

That April evening in St. Peter's Square, it became clear to me that, age notwithstanding, Cardinal Ratzinger was no less a member of the "JPII generation" than any of us youngsters were. With us he missed John Paul the Great terribly, and with us he loved him more than ever before and looked to him in a new and profound way as his spiritual father and guide. The new pope was one of us!

There could have been no better possible outcome to the papal election. St. Peter's Square and the entire Church had been anointed in a powerful and visible way with a Pentecost grace of joy, mercy, peace and thanksgiving. We had trusted the Lord that in taking John Paul II away from us he had a plan that was for our good. In a way that seemed too good to be true, the Lord had delivered. And isn't that always how it works when we open ourselves to the promptings of the Holy Spirit? *Habemus Papam—Deo gratias!*

Even in death, John Paul II continues to have an impact on young people, as the following two testimonies demonstrate. Those who have venerated the relics of the late Holy Father have felt a grace and power move through them calling them to follow Christ without fear.

Overwhelmed With Joy

Rachel Kolbeck, Wisconsin

Pope John Paul II died at 9:37 PM on Saturday, April 2, 2005. He was eighty-four years old. I was privileged to be in Rome when he died. I was present when he gave his last Easter blessing; I prayed under his window the night he was dying; I waited in line for ten hours to view his body in St. Peter's Basilica; and in 2006 I visited his tomb. Each one of these times I knew I was in the presence of someone who loved us young people and never underestimated us.

Pope John Paul II gave me a real understanding of what it is like to be and live close to our Lord and to really know him. The pope taught us about forgiveness, hard work, love, faith and dedication to youth. I thank God I was in Rome during this time, and I thank him for all of the things our deceased Holy Father has taught us.

The first time I saw Pope John Paul II was on Sunday, March 27, 2005, at his last Easter Blessing. He was up in his window, and I was down in St. Peter's Square along with thirty students and teachers from my school and thousands of other people. It was a beautiful sunny day in Rome, and there were so many people waiting in St. Peter's Square. Seeing all of these devout and holy people reminded me that we are not alone in our faith. There are so many people out in the world who believe in the same things we do and are fighting to keep the same faith alive. It is a joyous and overwhelming experience to receive such a reminder.

When the pope appeared at his window, he tried to speak, but he was in such pain he couldn't raise his voice above a whisper, so with great difficulty he raised his hand and made the Sign of the Cross. I was standing next to a friend, and when the pope appeared at his window, she turned and looked at me and said, "Rachel, that's a real live saint!" She was completely right. A living saint was standing right above us and he was blessing us. I was overwhelmed with joy and amazement, although I was a little sad because he was in so much pain. He went through tremendous pain to raise his hand to bless us. This was the only time I ever saw Pope John Paul II while he was alive.

The second time I was close to Pope John Paul II was on Friday night, April 1, 2005. My high school group was staying at a convent, and when we heard the pope was dying, we took taxis right away to St. Peter's Square and knelt and prayed for him. This was a sad time, because we all loved this pope and he was going to be leaving us.

There was chaos in St. Peter's Square that night. People were everywhere, news reporters were snapping photographs, and people were singing and praying and crying for the pope. We didn't pay very much attention to any of them; we were all concerned about our beloved father who was in so much pain. We all loved him and wanted him to stay with us. He had been the pope our entire lives. No one wanted him to die, but we knew that if it was God's will it was necessary and good.

I saw the body of Pope John Paul II on Monday, April 4, 2005, after waiting in line in the hot sun for ten hours in order to pay my respects. We went into the basilica silently. As we were walking down the aisle I started to cry. This was the man who had been pope all my life. He was a sweet man, who loved and believed in the youth of the world. I will never forget the man lying there in the center of St. Peter's who gave so much of his time and energy for Catholics around the world. I took a picture as I went by, and that picture will always remind me of Pope John Paul II and everything he was, everything he did and stood for.

After we passed him, I tried to walk back to see him again, but the guards wouldn't let me. This was probably the most moving time I saw him. It was well worth waiting in the sun for ten hot hours to see this wonderful and beautiful man. He didn't underestimate youth. He believed in youth with all his heart. He expected great things from us.

In the spring of 2006, I visited his tomb. While there, all of the memories I had of Pope John Paul II were running and replaying through my mind like they were actually happening. I missed him, his sweet face and his beautiful, loving smile. But I was thankful for all the things he taught us. It was great to be able to go back and visit him again. It is also comforting to know that he is up in heaven with God watching over every one of us.

He modeled faith, hard work, love and forgiveness to us. He was an extremely faithful man. He loved God and was a prime example of how to be and act. We learn hard work from him because even when he was eighty-three years old, he was a busy man, with meetings and things to do. On an average day he probably did more than we do, and we are a lot younger than he was. He taught us to forgive our enemies by forgiving the man who tried to kill him. Actions speak louder than words.

Saying Good-Bye

Jacqueline Dickmann, Wisconsin

In the spring of 2006 I went to Rome for the first time on a high school trip. My most vivid memory of the trip is not of the Colosseum or of any statues, gardens, buildings, or anything like that. Instead, I remember standing in front of the tomb of John Paul II for a few precious seconds while hastily taking a picture. It felt like a much longer time than it really was. There were people all around me, and guards were forcing people to keep moving. I was one of the luckier ones who got a really good picture of his tomb.

I'll probably never forget several things about those few seconds: the inscription on the tomb itself, the picture of the little girl that was next to the tomb, the rose next to it, and the face of the guard who was pushing traffic along three feet away from it. As I walked out of the grottoes beneath St. Peter's Basilica, where the tombs of the popes are, I stood outside and just looked at my picture. I remember not quite knowing what I was feeling; all I knew was that I had changed. To this day, I don't know what it is—but I know it's real, and that in time God will show me more. I remember crying that last day after the Mass while saying good-bye to St. Peter's Basilica and the tomb of John Paul II, possibly never to come back. Saying good-bye was so hard.

John Paul II was a pope who really understood youth. He has influenced all young people who are Catholic—and many who are not—in some way or another, whether they realize it or not. The idea for World Youth Day would never have happened if God hadn't instilled in him the conviction that today's young people are called to holiness no less than adults. His death would not have been such an extraordinary world event if it wasn't for the amazing love for people that he brought to every corner of the globe.

Without Pope John Paul II many vocations would never have been heard, many souls would have been lost and the Church would not have the same life that it does now. In a time when much of the world has given up on today's youth, Pope John Paul II maintained his belief that young people could have just as caring, loving and zealous hearts as adults, if not more so. It was his firm, God-given belief in young people that changed the Church and began the great "youth revolution" that is continuing today.

Epilogue

"You are witnesses of these things" (Luke 24:48). Our Lord sent forth the apostles when he had completed the course of his earthly life, to share his message and to tell others about him. The content of the apostolic preaching and witness was in large part telling stories about Jesus to those who had never met him—all of the amazing things he had said and done, what he was like and how he had touched their lives.

In an analogous way, a similar witness has been occurring in the very brief time since Pope John Paul the Great made his final journey to the house of the Father. During his life he gathered us around him as witnesses of the love of Jesus Christ. With us he was a disciple of Christ, but it was primarily from encountering him— John Paul II—seeing his example and listening to his words—that we learned what it means to follow Jesus as his disciple and to trust him completely. If that was true of the entire life of John Paul II, how much more was it true of the profoundly spiritual time of his death and burial in Rome in April, 2005?

Three weeks before the Holy Father died, I received a new assignment from my bishop and was asked to serve as a pastor back home in my diocese. The morning after the solemn installation of Pope Benedict on Sunday, April 24, I departed Rome and shipped all my belongings back to Nebraska. A few weeks later I became the pastor of two tiny rural parishes, Assumption Church of Dwight and St. Wenceslaus Church of Bee. I have not returned to Rome since.

Every Wednesday night at 8:00 PM, the youth of my parishes gather for what I have named the "JP2 Club." The walls of the room where we meet are covered with pictures of John Paul the Great. There is one of him as a young priest at the Acropolis in Athens wearing "cool" black sunglasses and a cassock, another of him skiing in the Italian Alps, yet another of him hiking in the mountains, staff in hand, on one of his summer vacations. Another one is a close-up of him holding a monstrance and blessing the crowds on one of his many pilgrimages, still another shows him pointing playfully and joyfully with his index finger straight into the camera: "You," he seems to be saying, "are called to follow Christ!" On a shelf in the corner there is a framed and autographed photo of me being blessed by him with my family at the Vatican in 2003. And on a side wall there is a framed shot of Pope Benedict at the moment of his election, hands raised in the air and beaming joyfully.

Every Wednesday the teenagers of my parish pile in

for the weekly meeting of the JP2 Club and eat all the food I put in front of them. Two seminarians also attend and help me in leading the group. We laugh, we talk, we might read the Bible or pray part of the rosary, we might sing a song or hear about one of the saints, we might read a little of the *Catechism* and discuss it, we might do a skit about some aspect of the faith and then relate it to the struggles of being a Christian and a high school student in today's world.

And inevitably, even if I don't plan on doing it, somehow John Paul II comes up in the course of the evening's conversation. I tell them what he said to us when I was with him, I talk about what it was like to have been at World Youth Day with him or to have lived Holy Week in Rome. We have bonfires, canoe trips and other outings that are just for fun. We are saving up for a pilgrimage to Rome where, among other things, we hope to pray at John Paul's tomb. In a very imperfect and weak way, I try to be for them the father John Paul II was as a young priest to the youth of Poland. He is my hero and the one whom I constantly strive to imitate in my priesthood.

These teenagers are the next generation after mine. They never saw John Paul personally, and they don't remember him as anything other than frail and old. When I first arrived and asked them what they knew about him they weren't even sure what country he came from. And so I tell them about him, all the time. I so wish they could have been with him in person as I was so privileged to have been. But since they can't do that now, I tell them about him, again and again and again.

The early Church had a word for this method of forming disciples. They called it "Tradition"—the handing over of the faith. Jesus sent the twelve apostles, then the apostles told men like Timothy and Titus and Ignatius and Polycarp about Jesus. They in turn told others. Down the centuries this living Tradition has been passed on. It can only be done in person, and it consists primarily of spreading the gospel by word of mouth and the witness of one's life, transforming each other through personal encounter.

John Paul sent me in the name of Christ, and now I am his apostle, one who has been sent by both of them—by Jesus through the joyful and courageous witness of John Paul II—to proclaim the good news of salvation. John Paul renewed a living, contagious Spirit in the Church by his pontificate. I personally witnessed it, and now it is my mission to spread it even to the ends of the earth. It is the Spirit of Jesus Christ, truly risen from the dead, who dwells in our midst.

I will end where it all began for me, with the words of Pope John Paul the Great to me and to my generation at World Youth Day 1993 in Denver. He sent us as missionaries then with these powerful words, and they have been ringing in my ears ever since:

Epilogue

Beloved young people:…

At this stage of history, the liberating message of the Gospel of Life has been put into your hands. And the mission of proclaiming it to the ends of the earth is now passing to your generation. Like the great Apostle Paul, you too must feel the full urgency of the task: "Woe to me if I do not evangelize."

…

Do not be afraid to go out on the streets and into public places, like the first Apostles who preached Christ and the Good News of salvation in the squares of cities, towns and villages. This is no time to be ashamed of the Gospel. It is the time to preach it from the rooftops.[1]

We have heard you, Holy Father! And we will strive, with the help of your prayers, to be faithful to Christ as you were and are. Saint John Paul the Great, pray for us! Obtain for us from Christ the grace to be the saints of the third millennium. And know that we will never forget how much you loved us.

Notes

Preface

1. Pope Benedict XVI, Papal Installation Mass, April 24, 2005, www.ewtn.com.

Chapter One: The Vigil

1. John Paul II spoke these words (my translation) to the young people gathered in prayer for him in St. Peter's Square on the night before he died. Reported by Dr. Joaquin Navarro Valls, Corriere della Sera, April 4, 2005, www.corriere.it.
2. G.K. Chesterton, "A Defence of Heraldry," from *The Defendant* (London: Johnson, 1902), www.dur.ac.uk.
3. Joseph Ratzinger, Homily delivered at the funeral of Pope John Paul II, April 8, 2005, www.ewtn.com.

Chapter Two: The Passing

1. John Paul II, *Dives in Misericordia,* November 30, 1980, VIII:15, www.vatican.va.

Chapter Three: Divine Mercy Outpoured

1. Maria Faustina Kowalska, *Diary: Divine Mercy in My Soul,* 3rd ed. (Stockbridge, Mass.: Marian Press, 2001), p. 139.
2. Kowalska, no. 1224, p. 440.
3. Kowalska, p. 440.
4. Kowalska, p. 440.